AF568127

AQUATIC BIODIVERSITY

AQUATIC BIODIVERSITY

Edited by

Dr. Lingaraj Patro

Professor & Head

Deptt. of Zoology & Biotechnology

K.B.D.A.V. College, Nirakarpur, Khurda

(Orissa) (India)

DISCOVERY PUBLISHING HOUSE PVT. LTD.

NEW DELHI-110 002

Published by:
Tilak Wasan

DISCOVERY PUBLISHING HOUSE PVT. LTD.
4383/4B, Ansari Road, Darya Ganj
New Delhi-110 002 (India)
Phone : +91-11-23279245, 43596064-65
Fax : +91-11-23253475
E-mail : discoverypublishinghouse@gmail.com
namitwasan9@gmail.com
sales@discoverypublishinggroup.com
web : www.discoverypublishinggroup.com

***Reprinted:* 2018**

***First Edition:* 2010**

ISBN: 978-81-8356-637-7

Aquatic Biodiversity

Printed at:
Infinity Imaging Systems
Delhi

Preface

The earth with its complex environment abounds in millions and millions of biological diversified organisms represented by variety of species, eco-races or strains with its own genetic identity well linked with each other for their long-term sustainable existence. Thus, biodiversity provides the basis for life on earth. Since water is the habitat of legions of organisms and forms the biggest ecosystem of the biosphere, it is indispensable to present some topics on aquatic plants and animals. Hence, this volume on aquatic biodiversity. Aquatic biome constitutes about 75 per cent of the earth's surface. It is usually classified in to two basic regions i.e., fresh water (ponds, some lakes and rivers) and Marine (ocean, lakes and estuaries). Fresh water biomes have suffered mainly from pollution. Ponds and lakes have varied zones such as littoral zone, limnetic zone and profundal zone. Aquatic biodiversity includes all organisms living in fresh water and marine water. These aquatic organisms contribute to (I) food (II) Medicine and other industrial use of mankind. Use of fish and growing of fish and fishing have been a common practice in many countries since time immemorial. Due to advancement of science many techniques have been invented and is studied separately as aquaculture technology providing necessary technology to the farmers for the benefits of the society in particular. These are namely: (i) Food production-particularly of animal protein obtained for common as well as effluent people; (ii) Providing new employment opportunity to rural people thereby checking migration of people; (iii) Improving economic condition of rural people in particular through integrated projects; (iv) Earning foreign exchange; (v) Utilization of waste food and organic wastes for food production; (vi) Agro-industrial development through marketing of fishery products, feeds and equipments for aquaculture, sea weed culture for production of marine colloids, pearl oyster culture, etc. Keeping in view the importance of aquatic organisms in shaping the nation's economy the present volume intends to highlight some important aspects of aquatic biodiversity.

"Aquatic Biodiversity" contains selected articles by eminent professors, academicians, researchers and scientists of different parts of India and abroad pertaining to a variety of issues and dimensions of aquatic biodiversity. It is expected that this book will profusely assist the policy makers, researchers, conservation and management personnel and general readers for policy implications.

Dr. Lingaraj Patro

Acknowledgements

I can't but gratefully acknowledge my indebtedness to all those who have extended unstinting assistance in the successful accomplishment of this noble work. It will be a serious blunder if I forget to mention some of my colleagues Prof. Dr. S.N. Padhi, Vice-Principal, Prof. Sarat Chandra Mishra, Head, Department of English, and Dr. Suresh Chandra Rath, Head, Dept. of Chemistry, K.B.D.A.V. College, Nirakarpur for their ardent encouragement and beacon-guidance in bringing out this work. Last but not least my heart felt gratitude to my wife knows no bounds for her unblemished co-operation.

I am also much beholden to Mr. Tilak Wasan, Managing Director, Discovery Publishing House Pvt. Ltd., New Delhi for publishing the work in a record time.

Dr. Lingaraj Patro

Contents

1

May Vanadium Contamination Influence the Filtration and Oxygen Consumption Rates of Mud Cockle *Cerastoderma lamarki* (Mollusca, Bivalvia)?

Arash Javanshir[1]

ABSTRACT

Petroleum exploration in the continental shelf of the Caspian sea shores may has a nuisible impact on bivalve communities living in this region of the sea. Petroleum leakage can cause heavy metal pollution among benthic communities, especially filter feeder bivalves such as mud cockle *Cerastoderma lamarki* of the Caspian Sea closed system. One of the markers of this group of metallic pollution may be the Vanadium contamination. Thus short-term oxygen consumption and filtration rate experiments were conducted to evaluate the response of mud cockle *Cerastoderma lamarki* when contaminated by the Vanadium heavy metal. In this work we have measured

1. University of Tehran, Faculty of Natural Resources.
E-mail: arashjavanshir@hotmail.com

metabolic activities of bivalves to determine this particular aspect of the host – heavy metal interactions. We have used the Vanadium contamination as a factor which can alter the metabolic rates of its host: the mud cockle *Cerastoderma lamarki* from South Caspian Sea basin (Iranian coasts). This is the first study of this type. Results showed that oxygen consumption and pumping rate of contaminated cockles decreased in comparison with that of healthy ones. This decrease in specific pumping rate is mainly due to the infection and disease state which can provoke the decrease in oxygen need of the animal which reduces the true metabolic activities. The results show that pumping rate is related to the initial concentration of Vanadium with greater contamination associated with lower oxygen consumption. We also demonstrate that *cockles contaminated with Vanadium are* capable of oxygen consumption regulation. The consumption rate is maintained below 0,3 µmol O_2 min^{-1} g^{-1} FDW (Flesh Dry Weight) in all external oxygen concentrations experimented. Our results also show that contamination of cockles with *this metal can* reduce the stress associated with transport and manipulation of the hosts.

Key words: Caspian sea; filtration rate; respiration rate; *Cerastoderma lamarki*; heavy metals; oil pollution.

INTRODUCTION

The Caspian Sea is a landlocked body of water bordered by five countries, Russia, Iran, Kazakhstan, Turkmenistan, and Azerbaijan, all but one of which (Iran) constituted part of the former Soviet Union. Though they differ markedly in size, population, ethnic composition, they share the common interest of maximizing the substantial energy wealth of the Caspian basin, and dealing successfully with the environmental issues that affect the explorations for, production, refining, and transport of energy resources. The production of energy, particularly oil, can cause the pollution due to oil spill which is unavoidable. This kind of pollution enhances the vulnerability of food chain in the Caspian Sea living resources ecosystem. Among them, macrobentic organisms at the primary consumers of primary production may suffer more than others. The bivalve's oxygen consumption rate has raised interest for a long time because of their role in trophic chain as a first consumer of primary production. This interest comes from more interests in particle retention in the exact sciences or its interest in aquaculture or still as biomarkers in understanding the impacts of pollution on benthic communities. In practice it has been proved that it is difficult to measure it in conditions where the animal is relatively free from constraint. The estimation of oxygen consumption and filtration rate is important in a number of aspects:

(i) in pollution studies where it is an indicator of the animal's reaction to its environment;

(ii) in aquaculture, for the prediction of optimal flow of water required; and

(iii) in estimating the species survival in nature when it is confronted with stress factors such as pollution.

Most bivalve molluscs pump the ambient water through the pallial cavity by means of ciliated gills. The muco-ciliary mechanism of the gill in many bivalves is modified to collect suspended nutritious particles and convey them to the mouth (Jorgensen, 1990). These animals pump excessive volumes of water in comparison to the respiration requirements. However, in suspension feeders, the gill filaments have become greatly elongated and folded on themselves, effectively increasing the exchange surface area. The bivalve pump configuration is made of inhalant and exhalant areas (Siphons) of relatively small sizes, leading to a chamber separated by a large area of gill bearing numerous ciliated slits or pores between gill filaments which act as series of pumps. The oxygen expense of pumping (Collier, 1959; Dejours, 1972) is one possible method to compare the efficiency of various gill and siphon configurations between bivalves. However, a large variety of other methods have been proposed (Jones & Allen, 1986; Byrne *et al.*, 1990; Eriksen & Iversen, 1997; *Bayne et al.*, 1987; Beninger *et al.*, 1991; Visman, 1990; De Villiers *et al.*, 1989). Our knowledge of the physiological responses of bivalves in natural population hardly results from direct observations in the wild but is usually deducted from extrapolations of results obtained in the laboratory. In order to establish the legitimacy of such extrapolations, measurements in high controlled conditions are needed. In spite of many controlled conditions such as temperature, salinity, etc., there is a variety of results among the measures on filtration or respiration rates for the same species in the literature (Fig. 1.7). Thus, data about reasons of the variety of measures are not clearly known. These variations may be the result of physiological modifications in response to the factors which may have been ignored, such as the potential effect of contamination by oil pollution on oxygen consumption. Taking this factor into account may be important for bivalve modelling studies in which generally the gains and losses of animal is accounted independent from the contamination factor.

In the present study, *in vitro* measurement of respiration and filtration rates of *C. lamarki from south Caspian Sea basin* were carried out on healthy animals and on individuals contaminated artificially with *Vanadium as marker of oil contamination*. Respiration measurements were performed on the individuals using a method involving collection and adaptation of animals prior to the measurements and two groups of healthy and contaminated animals were compared. In addition, the oxygen consumption of the contaminated Hepato-pancreas tissue mass itself was measured and the two oxygen consumption rates were compared. Such comparisons have never been performed so far.

MATERIALS AND METHODS

Oxygen and filtration rates of cockles were measured separately. The groups used for both measurements came from the same site of Turkmen-Bender, in south Caspian Sea coasts (Fig. 1.1). This site is located in the eastern part of the bay of Gorgan (south east of the Caspian sea, 36°48′ N; 53°06′ E and is protected by the Ashuradeh sand banks. Previous pre-samplings performed to establish the spatial distribution of cockles in the bay show that the cockles of this site are not infected by any pesticides.

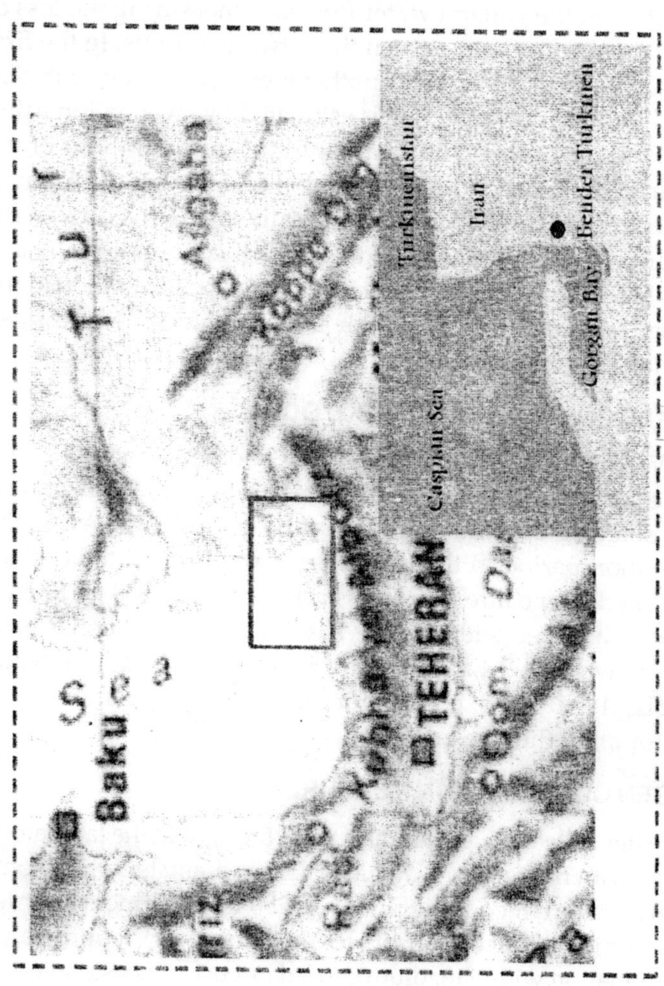

Fig. 1.1: The Gorgan bay and Bender Turkmen situation in the south-east of this bay and the Caspian Sea. At this site the cockles were not contaminated by Vanadium heavy metal.

There are two methods to predict oxygen consumption of a bivalve in an *in vitro* experimentation: either by measuring the rate of removal oxygen concentration from input to output of seawater through a container, or by separating the exhalant current from the general water flow and measuring the loss of oxygen concentration between these two mediums. In the first 'indirect' method, an algal or another inert particle concentration is used and the pumping rate is estimated by an equation using the difference between input and output concentrations of the system. In the second 'direct method' (Ege & Krogh, 1914; James & Allen, 1986), a rubber cone (or catheter) is fixed over the exhalant organ of the shell and this leads the pumped water to a separate overflow. The difference of oxygen concentration in the pumped water and in input water is used to measure the oxygen retention by the animal.

COCKLE CONTAMINATION PROTOCOL

Vanadium oxide (V_2O_5) was used in order to infect a group of 50 cockles. Cockles of the same size range (28.9 mm, σ: 0.1) were selected for the contamination procedure. After the acclimation period in the laboratory, five group of ten cockles established in one litre recipients each containing 800 ml filtered seawater saturated with oxygen. The initial concentration in each recipient was 0.2, 0.4, 0.6, 0.8, and 1.0 $mg.l^{-1}$ of vanadium oxide well dissolved. The exposure duration for contamination was 5 hour for all of the five groups.

OXYGEN CONSUMPTION MEASUREMENTS

After collection, the animals were brought to the laboratory, washed with filtered sea water in order to eliminate the epibionts and then maintained individually in 250 ml containers in order to beginning of acclimation to the laboratory conditions. Contamination with Vanadium carried out using a basic solution of 1 $mg. ml^{-1}$ as mentioned above. Individuals of the two groups of contaminated and healthy cockles were then marked and were maintained in filtered sea current water during 48 h to allow the clearance of the gut contents and acclimatisation again after contamination, to the laboratory conditions. Temperature was maintained at 20 ± 1° C. In each measurement, two groups of cockles (healthy and contaminated) were selected with the closest possible mean size and brought into the oxygen consumption glass chamber of 0.75 ml Vol. (Fig. 1.2), measurements were repeated for 10 couples of cockles (healthy and infected). The water entering this chamber consisted of filtered sea water (0.45 µm), saturated with oxygen in normoxia conditions (PO_2 = 21 kPa), and was conducted through stainless steel pipes of 0.5 mm inside∅. The pumping action was generated with a Braun-Melsungen pump at a constant rate of 300 µl. min^1. The position of cockles in the chamber was designed to resemble natural condition in the sediment remaining in vertical position when inhalant and exhalent siphons directed at the top of animal. This was achieved by using an oyster culture net of 5 mm mesh size (Fig. 1.2). Each experiment on a single cockle lasted for 16 minutes during which, four samples of 5 ml of water from the entry and exit pipes were re-sampled with a glass syringe. The oxygen concentration of each sample (entrance or exit) was then measured using an oxygen electrode (Clark Radiometer E 5046, modified in laboratory for these measurements). Each time, the measurement was repeated four times from sub-samples 1 ml volume each. The results of each cockle presented the averages of the four measurements. Oxygen consumption measures were converted into MO_2 unity (µmol. O_2. min^{-1}), following the equation proposed by Dejours (1981):

$$MO_2 = V.\ \alpha\, wO_{2.} (PeO_2 - PsO_2)$$

In which,

MO_2:	oxygen consumption per time (µmol. min^{-1})
V:	water entrance flux in the chamber (ml. min^{-1})
αwO_2:	oxygen solubility coefficient in sea water (µmol. L^{-1}. kPa^{-1}), (11, 12 in our case)
PeO_2 & PsO_2:	oxygen partial pressure in input and output water of the chamber (kPa)

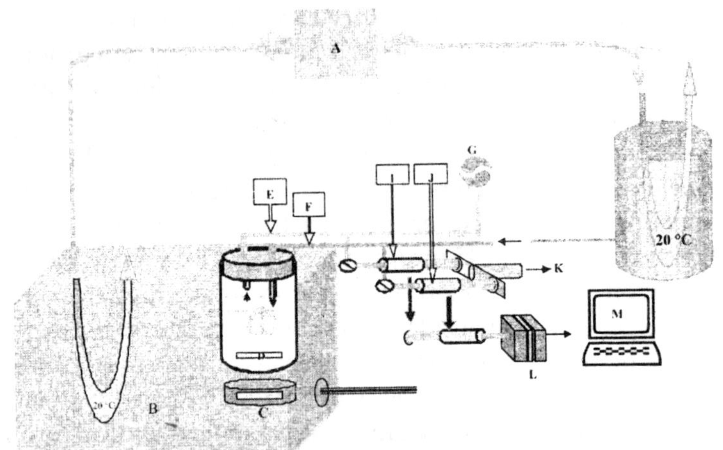

Fig. 1.2: Respiration measurement unit. *A & B: thermostatic baths of 20° C, G: peristaltic pump that evacuates the seawater through tube E. C & D are stirrer with its magnet bar. Each sample (I & J) is taken through the stainless steel tubes (E & F) from measurement chamber that is suspended in thermostatic bath (in order to lessen any shock). In the chamber the cockle is situated on an plastic, 5 mm mesh size filet. Finally oxygen content of each sample was measured by radiometer (L).*

After each measurement the cockle was dissected. The hepato-pancreas tissue was entirely removed from the cockle body and separated. The flesh weight of each of these separated tissues was immediately measured with a 10^{-4} g precision scale. Their dry weight was measured after 48 h in a 50°C oven.

In addition, oxygen consumption of infected tissue before the dissection was examined in normoxia ranging from 14 to 21 kPa. In this case, all of the hepato-pancreas tissue separated just after the oxygen consumption experiment of the entire cockle and this tissue was suspended in 5 ml oxygen saturated filtered sea water within a glassware syringe following the method described in Quetin & Mickel (1978). After ten minutes (lethal time for exhausting oxygen concentration), oxygen measurement was carried out by vertical injection of

1 ml of suspending liquid extract into the oxygen electrode during two minutes. Injections were repeated four times, and the water in; the syringe containing the suspended hepato-pancreas tissue was renewed four times after each measurement. At each time, both of the entire hepato-pancreas masses were examined in the same manner. The oxygen consumption of this mass was calculated from equation:

$$MO_2 \,.\, B^{-1} = V \,.\, \alpha\, wO_2 \,.\, (PO_2 \text{ at } t_0 - PO_2 \text{ at } t_{10\,min}) \,.\, B^{-1}$$

where,

MO_2:	is the oxygen consumption per time unit (µmol. min $^{-1}$)
B:	dry weight of hepato-pancreas mass (contaminated or healthy) (g)
V:	volume of suspension at t_0 (ml)
αwO_2:	oxygen solubility coefficient in sea water which is related to salinity and temperature (µmol,. L $^{-1}$. kPa $^{-1}$), (11, 12 in our case)
PO_2 at t_0 &:	$t_{10\,min}$ oxygen partial pressure at the beginning and at the end of the 10 minutes incubation. (ml)

Biometric measurements and fresh and dry weight of this mass were then performed.

Filtration Rate Measurements

Filtration rates were estimated using a 75 ml filtration glass chamber, in a thermostatic bath at 20°C as described above. The chamber was maintained suspended in the thermostatic bath (see Fig. 1.2) to prevent any hazardous shock due to resonance of chamber. Filtered seawater with added algae concentration of *Skeletonema costatum* (10^4 cells. ml $^{-1}$) was pumped through a 500 µm pipe into the chamber. Outflow from the chamber was carried out through a 1 mm (interior diameter) tube. After a 24 hours adaptation time, 5 ml samples were taken every 60 minutes, 8 times from each cockle chamber simultaneously. Each time 5ml of filtered see water was added to maintain constant water level in the chamber. Determination of algae concentration in input and output overflow was made using a Coulter Counter with a 100 µm aperture size (Model ZI coulter). The filtration rate was calculated using the equation of Jorgensen (1990):

$$Vw = \frac{Ln(C_{t0}) - Ln(C_{t60})}{t.W}$$

where,

Vw: filtration rate (ml . min^{-1} . g^{-1} DW)

C_{t0} & C_{t60}: algae concentration before and after experiment (cell . ml^{-1})

W: weight g

t: experiment period (minute)

The application of this equation induces the acceptance of four hypotheses:

(i) the algae concentration decrease is merely due to bivalve filtration;

(ii) the filtration rate is constant during the short measurement time;

(iii) the retention efficiency is 100%;

(iv) The algal distribution in the media remains homogeneous during the experiment period.

The selection and adaptation period for starving conditions of 48 H before measurements starts, insure the high particle retention by the cockles following their starving state. At the end of each experiment, the chamber was examined and no algal accumulation on its walls was observed. The short laps of experiment time and the repetition of replicates have had to assume a constant filtration during experiments and among all the samples. In any case, the experiment running time was shorter than the gut passage time of *C. lamarki* calculated following to Hawkins *et al*'s. (1990) formula:

$$Y = 1{,}71\ X^{0{,}41 \pm 0{,}32}$$

where, Y is in hour and X in g FDW) which give us 68 minutes. The homogeneity of media in the chamber was insured by means of:

(i) the current created by animal;

(ii) the current created by input into the chamber; and

(iii) the magnetic stirrer beneath the chamber.

RESULTS

Biometric Aspects

The mean size of infected cockles was 28.9 mm (σ : 0.1) and that of the healthy ones was 29.0 mm (σ: 0.2). The difference in the mean size was not significant (*t*-test: $t = 0.3$; $p > 0.05$; DF = 21). Contrarily FDW (flesh dry weight) of infected cockles (0.31 g, $\sigma = 0.03$) was of 15% higher than that of healthy ones (0.19 g , σ : 0.02 t test). The average weight of extracted hepato-pancreas mass in both infected and healthy cockles was 0.171 g DW ($\sigma = 0.02$). The weight of healthy cockles (0.189 g DW σ : 0.02) was more important than contaminated ones without the hepato-pancreas mass (0.138 g DW σ : 0.02, this mass removed) but there was no significant difference between these values ($t = -1.55$; $p > 0.05$; df = 21).

Oxygen Consumption

Figure 1.3 shows the three different types of comparisons of oxygen consumption rates between contaminated and healthy animals as found in the literature.

(i) Comparison of fresh weight (FW);

(ii) Comparison of dry weight (DW), the most commonly used in literature;

(iii) Comparison of animal size.

The results (Fig. 1.3A) indicate that the average oxygen consumption rate of 29 mm healthy cockles is greater than that of infected ones. Although we have previously seen that the

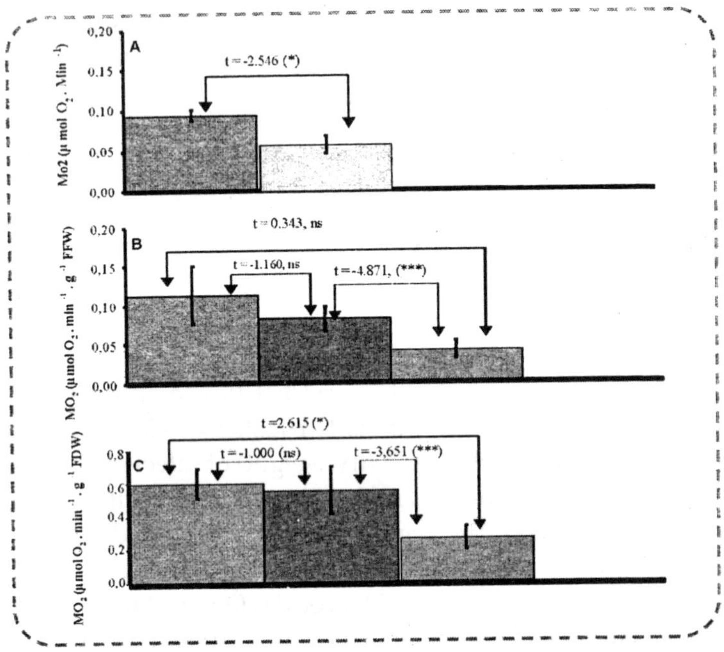

Fig. 1.3: A comparison between oxygen consumption values of contaminated cockles, healthy cockles and hepato-pancreas mass expressed in three different ways: A: per cockle, B: per flesh fresh weight; and C: per flesh dry weight. The bars show standard error of average. There is no significant difference - individually and fresh weight expressed comparisons- between healthy and contaminated cockles oxygen consumption. This difference is only significant when it is expressed in dry weight.

healthy cockles have a higher weight than the infected (hepato-pancreas mass removed), it is noticeable from Fig. 1.3B and 1.3C that the oxygen consumption of cockle divided by its weight *per se* is independent from the hepato-pancreas presence. Thus the lowest oxygen consumption of a cockle can be related to its less body weight. The cockle oxygen consumption is also related to contamination intensity as shown on Fig. 1.4. The greater the initial infection concentration in proportion to body weight, the less the oxygen consumption will be. This consumption approaches values near to 0.01 µmol. It can be estimated that beyond this proportion of infected weight, the cockle reaches a lethal stage with almost all of its body weight consisting of *high infected tissue*.

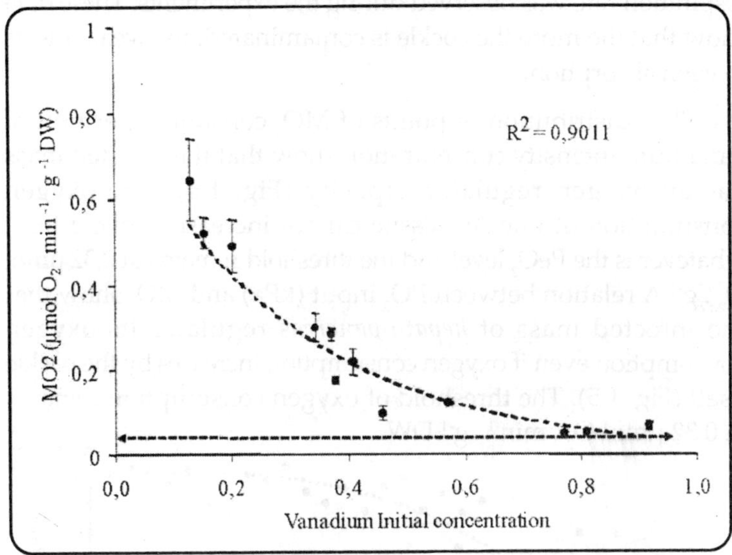

Fig. 1.4: Relation between oxygen consumption rate (in ordinate axis) and contamination ratio (Hepato-pancreas mass/cockle weight) in abscissa.

Figure shows that above 92% contamination (horizontal pointed line) of the cockle enter in a lethal stage following to decrease of oxygen consumption.

The results of contaminated hepato-pancreas mass oxygen consumption show that, contrary to what is commonly accepted in the literature, where the healthy state of animals has not taken in account in most of experiments, and for example internal parts of molusks such as the hepato-pancreas has not any aerobic metabolism (Cassier *et al.* 1998), the oxygen consumption changes because of acute infection by the vanadium was not null. Here, we observe that *the hepato-pancreas tissue itself* consumes 0.11µmol $O_2 . g^{-1}$ DW, σ : 0.01, which approximately represents 20% of the cockle oxygen consumption. It is clear that the mass extracted from cockle body was not a uniform mass and consisted of different organs, and perhaps a few cockle internal tissues. A negative correlation between contamination intensity and respiration rate was observed during the experiments. These data show that the more the cockle is contaminated, the weaker is its oxygen absorption.

The distribution of points of MO_2 consumed per unit of vanadium intensity concentration show that the infected mass has an oxygen regulator capacity (Fig. 1.5). The oxygen consumption of infected tissue cannot increase above a limit whatever is the PeO_2 level and the threshold remains at 0,32 µmol $O_2 . g^{-1}$ A relation between PO_2 input (kPa) and MO_2 show that the infected mass of *hepato-pancreas* regulates its oxygen consumption even if oxygen consumption increases by the cockle itself (Fig. 1.5). The threshold of oxygen consumption remains at 0,32 µmol $O_2 . min^{-1} . g^{-1}$ DW.

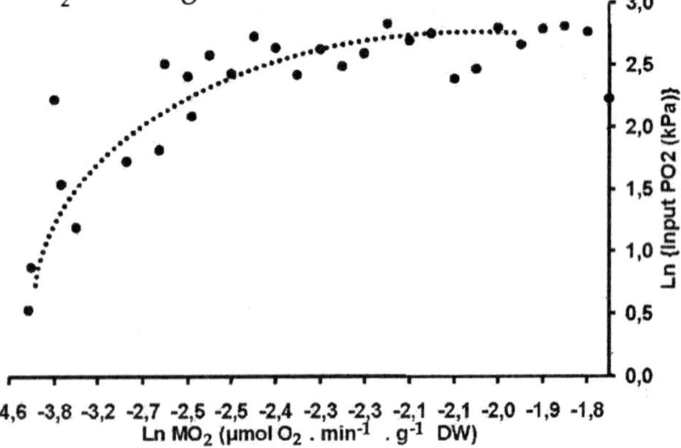

Fig. 1.5: (ln × ln) Points distribution of hepato-pancreas mass respiration measurements.

It is observed that this tissue mass requires an oxygen amount for its consumption up to a level which is limited by 0.32 µmol $O_2 . g^{-1}$ FDW.

Filtration Rate

The results of filtration rates of cockles at 20° C show that there is an individual variability between the replicates varying from 10 to 250 ml. min^{-1}. g^{-1} in the healthy group. The results of two series of measurements in October 2005 and August 2006 show that there was not any significant difference between the series of data one time they are acclimated to the laboratory conditions. The average being 78 ± 10 ml . min^{-1} . g^{-1} DW. In the Fig. 1.6, in order to show in a better way, we have used percentages for the variations of this value between 10 and 250 ml . min^{-1} . g^{-1} DW. The infected cockles show a decrease of filtration rate below to 15,4 ml . min^{-1} . g^{-1} DW. Diagram 1.6 shows the distribution of the points observed during experiments. We can see that the cockles infected with *Vanadium* have a tight variation up to 1, 5 and does not exceed 31 ml . min^{-1}. g^{-1} DW.

DISCUSSION

Experimental Conditions Criticism

In this study we have used the breathing physiology of bivalves as a comparison between the responses or interactions in host-toxic ecology. We have focused on the aerobic metabolism – ventilation activity and contamination interactions, which has not been considered so far in the literatures of bivalve respiration and filtration rates studies.

All of the cockles observed in this study were transplanted to the laboratory in one time and one site. Considering that the collection of animals is a stress factor, a sufficient recovery period must be allowed prior to optimise the respiration rate. We have used this stress due to transport as a factor in order to aggravate the potential differences between contaminated and healthy individuals. The stress due to transport is a high filtration (and equally respiration) stimulus for the aquatic organisms (McMahon, 1985; Truchot, 1992; Legeay & Massabuau, 1999). Our results showed that with the same body size, a contaminated cockle consumes less oxygen than a healthy one in controlled

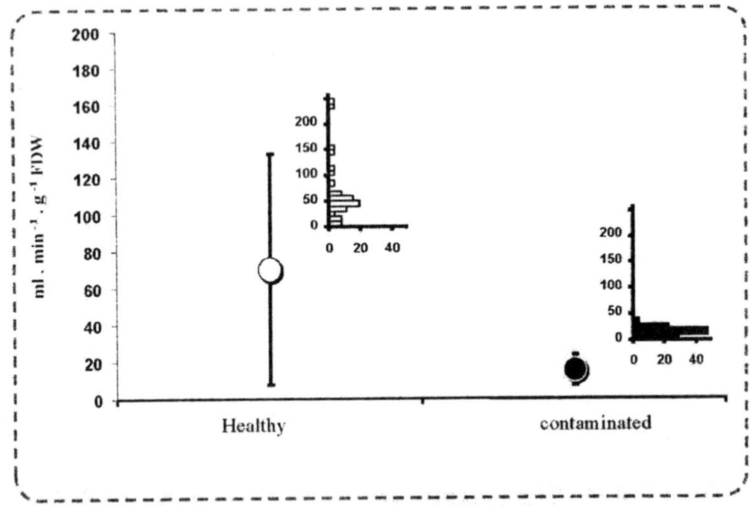

Fig. 1.6: Differences between healthy and infected cockles filtration rates in ordinate axis the clearance rate (ml. min^{-1}. g^{-1} FDW).

Bars show the standard error of average. Near to each average the value point's distribution is showed. Note the large variety of measures in healthy cockles compared to strict distribution of contaminated ones following to their infection state of intensity of vanadium. In the distribution diagram the abscissa shows the distribution percentage (0 to 50%) and ordinate axis is in ml. min^{-1}. g^{-1} FDW too.

conditions. Our results show that this difference is essentially due to the difference between infected tissue mass which present a disease state and cockle mass (with a same size, contaminated cockle has the same weight compared to a healthy one). Equally, we have showed that a hepato-pancreas tissue in suspention, which is considered to have an anaerobic metabolism (Grassé *et al.* 1970), consumes a lot of oxygen. Though internal tissues of a cockle (the hepato-pancreas as an example in our experiments) do not live in a very high oxygenated conditions, since the oxygenation state within a bivalve is at the weak values like the cases of *Modiolus demissus* (Booth & Mangum, 1978), *Anodonta cygnea* (Massabuau *et al.*, 1991), and *Corbicula fluminea* (Tran, 1997), but it can represent 20 % of its host oxygen consumption. It has a oxygen consumption regulation system and needs to an oxygen concentration between 2 to 4 kPa. Thus, whichever is its surrounding oxygen concentration; it needs to 4 kPa oxygen concentration approximately. This oxygen concentration is required to maintain alive the internal hepato-pancreas tissue.

For a contamination-host interaction, the cockle must pump the water to provide its needs which divided to any vital organs lodging in it. If we admit this hypothesis, the contaminated cockles must have oxygen consumption and filtration rates equal to the healthy ones if contaminated tissue consume equal to the uninfected tissue. But we have shown that this mass has requirements in oxygen lower than cockle tissue which does not exceed 20% of oxygen needed perhaps due to its disease state in the animal body. This interaction seems to be progressive as the contamination progress. Our results also show that in high contaminations with *Vanadium*, oxygen consumption approaches to 0,05 μmol O_2 . min^{-1} . g^{-1} DW which is a very low value compared to normal specific oxygen consumption rate of healthy ones. The respiration below this value may be lethal to host comparing to its high oxygen consumption in healthy conditions. Also as we have seen that the infected hepato-pancreas mass has an oxygen consumption regulator property, decrease in oxygen consumption in high contaminated cockles could conduct them into a lethal state. As we know, it is the first approach to the problem of water pollution influence on the pumping rate and it shows the difference of behaviour between two groups of the same species in the same conditions when the heavy metal contamination as a result of oil pollution in the sea is considered as a factor . A comparison of our data with many other literatures shows that variety it could not be estimated when past state of contaminations is not considered (Fig. 1.7).

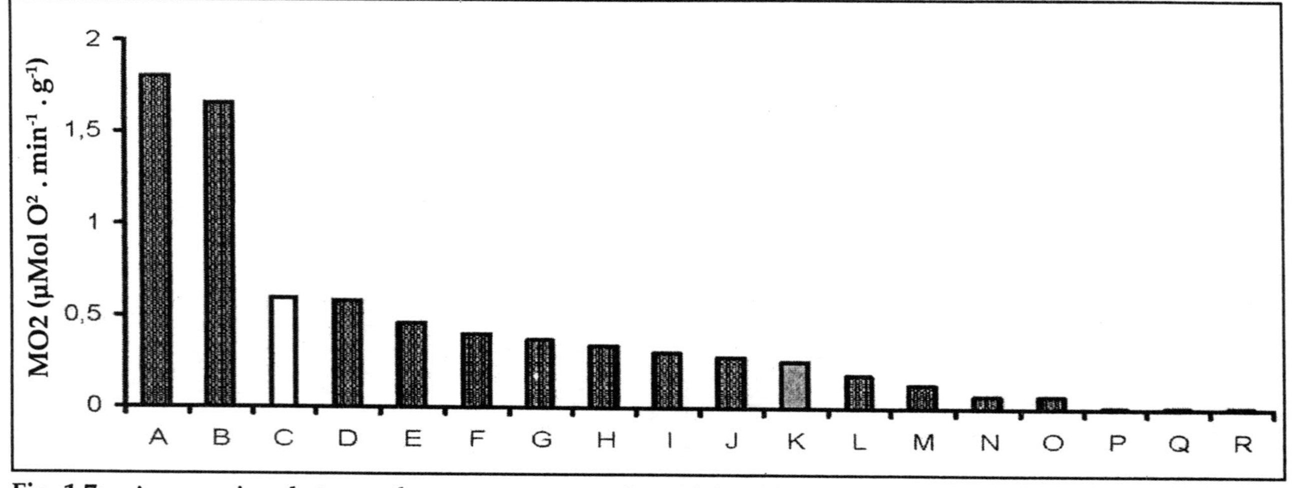

Fig. 1.7: A comparison between the oxygen consumption values of bivalve molluscs. As it is seen the big variety of measurements are explained by bivalve contamination state factor that is neglected. A: *Dreissena polymorpha* (Garton & Haag, 1991), B: *D. polymorpha* (Dorgelo & Smeenk, 1988), C: healthy *Cerastoderma lamarki* (this work), D: *Mytilus edulis* (Hamburger *et al*., 1983), E: *Mya truncata* (Bernard & Noakes, 1990), F: *Clinocardium nuttallii* (Bernard & Noakes, 1990), G: *Crassostrea gigas* (Bernard & Noakes, 1990), H: *M. edulis* (Bernard & Noakes, 1990), I: *Saxidomus giganteus* (Bernard & Noakes, 1990), J: *Chlamys hastata* (Bernard & Noakes, 1990), K: C. *Lamarki* infected by Vanadium heavy metal (this work), L: *Yoldia traciaeformis* (Bernard & Noakes, 1990), M: *Solemya reidi* (Bernard & Noakes, 1990), N: *C. edule* (Smaal, 1998), O: *Perna canaliculus* (Marsden & Weatherhead, 1998), P: *M. edulis* (Vismann, 1990), Q: *Anodonta cygnea* (Massabuau *et al*., 1991), R: *Corbicula fluminea* (Tran, 1997).

Also, results of filtration rate experiments show that, contaminated cockles have a pumping rate weaker than the healthy ones. The decrease in pumping rate is with a limitation in variety of filtration scale. These results indicate also that the cockles infected with Vanadium have disability of adaptation to laboratory conditions after artificial contamination, compared to healthy ones. The latter have pumped the water comfortably in a large variety contrarily to the infected ones. Regarding that the collection of animals from their natural habitat and their transport to the laboratory are factors of stress (Theed, 1963; Widdows, 1985; Massabuau & Legeay, 1999), our results showed that the contaminated cockles were also indifferent to this stress.

A comparison between both experiments of oxygen consumption as well as filtration rate measurements, suppose that the two actions are related with the *C. lamarki*. It pumps the water in order to capture the nutrient particle and insures its oxygen requirements. These two related factors are thus rather weaker in the contaminated cockles. These decreases are extremely related to their weak states because both groups of animals (healthy and artificially infected) were in the exactly same conditions. As it has been showed above, the high contamination with vanadium heavy metal leads to a state in which the cockle oxygen absorption become lower and lower.

In conclusion, we consider that the contamination by oil pollution and vanadium as a factor of this kind of pollutant may be one of the main factors influencing pumping rate and oxygen consumption in mud cockle *Cerastoderma lamarki* from south Caspian Sea basin.

REFERENCES

Bayne B.L., Hawkins A.J. S., and Navarro E. (1987). Feeding and Digestion by the Mussel *Mytilus edulis* L. (Bivalvia: Mollusca) in Mixture of Silt and Algal Cells at Low Concentrations. *J. Exp. Mar. Biol. Ecol.*, 111, pp. 1-22.

Beninger P.G., Le Pennec M. and Donval A. (1991). Mode of Particle Ingestion in Five Species of Suspension-feeding Bivalve Molluscs. *Mar. Biol.*, 108, 255-261.

Bernard F.R. & Noakes D.J. (1990). Pumping Rates, Water Pressures, and Oxygen use in Eight Species of Marine Bivalve Molluscs from British Columbia. *Can. J. Fish. Aquat. Sci.* 47, 1302-1306.

Byrne R.A., Gnaiger E., McMahon R. F. and Dietz T.H. (1990). Behaviornal and Metabolic Responses to Emersion and Subsequent Reimmersion in the Freshwater Bivalve *Corbicula Fluminea. Biol. Bull.*,178, 251-259.

Cassier P., Brugerolle G., Combes C., Grain J. and Raibaut A. (1998). *Le parasitisme. Un équilibre dynamique.* Masson, 365 pp.

Collier A. (1959). Some Observations on the Respiration of the American Oyster, *Crassostrea Virginica* (Gmelin). *Publ Inst. Mar. Sci. Univ. Tex.* 6, 92-108.

Dejours P. (1972). Comparison of Gas Transport by Convection Among Animals. *Respir. Physiol.* 14, 96-104.

Dejours P. (1981). *Principales of Comparative Respiratory Physiology.* Elsevier, 265.

Devilliers C.J., Allanson B.R. and Hodgson A.N. (1989). The Effect of Temperature on the Filtration Rate of *Solen Cylindraceus* (Hanley) (Mollusca: Bivalvia). *S. Afr. J. Zool.* 24, 11-17.

Dorgelo J. & Smeenk J. W. (1988). Contribution to the Ecophysiology of *Dreissena Polymorpha* (Pallas) (Mollusca: Bivalvia): Growth, Filtration Rate and Respiration. *Verh int Verein Limnol.*, 23, 2202-2208.

Ege R. & Krogh A. (1914). On the Relation Between the Temperature and the Respiratory Exchange in Fishes. *Int. Rev. ges. Hydrobiol. Hydrogr.* 7, 48-55.

Eriksen N.T. & Iversen J.J. L. (1997). On-line Determination of Respiration Rates of Aquatic Organisms in a Mono-phase Oxystat at Steady-state Dissolved Oxygen Tension. *Mar. Biol.*, 128, 181-189.

Garton D. W. & Haag W. R. (1991). Heterozygosity, Shell Length and Metabolism in the European Mussel *Dreissena Polymorpha*, from a Recently Established Population in Lake Erie.*Comp. Biochem. Physiol.*, 99, 45-48.

Grassé P.P., Poisson R. A. & Tuzet O. (1970). *Zoologie. I. Invertébrés.* 2e ed.,

Hamburger K., Møhlenberg F., Randlov A. & Riisgard H.U. (1983). Size, Oxygen Consumption and Growth in the Mussel *Mytilus Edulis. Mar. Biol.*, 75, 303-306.

Hawkins A. J. S., Navarro E., and Iglesias J. I. P. (1990). Comparative Allometries of Gut-passage Time, Gut Content and Metabolic Faecal Loss in *Mytilus edulis* and *Cerastoderma Edule. Mar. Biol.* 105, 197-204.

James H.D. and Allen J.R. (1986). Inhalant and Exhalant Pressures in *Mytilus Edulis* and *Cerastoderma Edule. J. Exp. Biol. Ecol.*, 98, 231-240.

Jórgensen C.B. (1990). *Bivalve Filter Feeding: Hydrodynamics, Bioenergetics, Physiology and Ecology.* Olsen & Olsen, Fredensborg, 140 p.

Legeay A. & Massabuau J. C. (1999). Blood Oxygen Requirements in Resting Crab *Carcinus Maenas* 24 hours after Feeding. *Can. J. Zool.*

McMahon, B.R. (1985). Functions and Functioning of Crustacean Hemocyanin. *In: Respiratory Pigments in Animals: Relation Structure Function.* J.N. Lamy, J.P. Truchot & R. Gilles. (eds). Springer, New York, 35-58.

Marsden I.D. & Weatherhead M. A. (1998). Effects of Aerial Exposure on Oxygen Consumption by the New Zealand Mussel *Perna Canaliculus* (Gmelin, 1791) from an Intertidal Habitat. *J. Exp. Mar. Biol. Ecol.*, 230, 15-29.

Massabuau J. C., Burtin B. & Wheathly M. (1991). How is O_2 Consumption Maintained Independent of Ambient Oxygen in Mussel *Anodonta Cygnea?. Respiration Physiology*, 83, 103-114.

Quetin L.B. , Mickel T. J. & Childress J.J. (1987). A Method for Simultaneously Measuring the Oxygen Consumption and Activity of Pelagic Crustaceans. *Comp. Biochem. Physiol.* 59 A: 263-266.

Smaal A.C. (1998). Food Supply and Demand of Bivalve Suspension Feeders in a Tidal System. *Thèse de doctorat, Université de Groningen.* 237 p.

Theede H. (1963). Experimentelle Untersuchungen über die Filtrationleistung der Meeresmuschel *Mytilus edulis* L. *Kieler Meeresforschungen*, 19, 20-41.

Tran D. (1997). Influence de l'oxygénation de l'eau et de l'activité respiratoire sur les mécanismes de bioaccumulation du cadmium chez le bivalve d'eau douce *Corbicula fluminea. DEA Université Bordeaux 1*, 23 p.

Truchot J.P. 1992. Respiratory Function of Arthropod Hemocyanins *In: Advances in Comparative and Environmental Physiology*, Vol 13. C.P. Mangum. (ed.), Springer, Heidelberg, 378-410.

Vismann B. (1990). Field Measurements of Filtration and Respiration Rates in *Mytilus edulis* L.: An Assessment of Methods. *Sarsia*, 75, 213-216.

Widdows J.P. (1985). Physiological Procedures. pp. 161-178 in Bayne B.L. (ed). *The Effects of Stress and Pollution on Marine Animals. Praeger Publishers*. New York.

2

Fish Diversity in Srikakulam District of Coastal Andhra Pradesh

Manjulatha C.[1]
Kiran Kumar Pappu[2]
Raju. D.V.S.N.[3]

ABSTRACT

Srikakulam District of Andhra Pradesh, which is situated on the east coast of India, is having long coastal region with Estuaries and Back waters. This coast is potential for fishery resources of both fin and shell fish. The diversity of fishery was studied in 20 important landing stations namely, Bharuva, Iskalapalem, Vajrapukotturu, Naupada, Bhavanapadu, Guppadapeta, Gullavanipeta, Rajaramapuram, Ampalam, Kalingapatnam, Bandaruvanipeta, Komaravanipeta, Mogadhara-padu, Srikurmam-Matschyalesam, Balaramapuram, Kunduvani-

1. Associate Professor Deptt. of Zoology, Andhra University, Visakhapatnam, 9-9-37/11, Rajiv Nagar, Sivaji palem, Visakhapatnam - 530017, Andhra Pradesh, (India).

peta, Mopasubandaru, Kallepalli, Dharmavaram-Matschyalesam and Koyyam in this district. The landing stations with more fish diversity were identified and the stations with high rates of landings were also reported in the present study. The total fishery of both fin and shell fish of commercial importance was reported altogether from 20 landing stations of Srikakulam district.

Key words: Diversity, fishery, Srikakulam District, landing stations.

INRODUCTION

Human beings are depending on the aquatic organisms for their food since a long time due to their great abundance and delicious taste. These aquatic organisms include both fresh and marine water, among which marine forms are of high value. Fishery is one of the oldest recorded sources of livelihood in India. During the past five decades, Indian fisheries has made tremendous progress, with the annual product increasing from 0.75 million tons in 1950 to 6.1 million tons in 2002, indicating over eight-fold increase during the period (Ayyappan and Jena, 2003). This is the outcome of research and development activities of various institutions. The fisheries sector plays a vital role in the Indian economy. It addresses various issues such as food and nutritional security, employment, livelihood support and socio-economic status of fishing communities. The sector provides employment and income to over 5 million fishers and fish farmers, majority of whom live in over 3600 coastal villages (Pillai and Pradeep, 2004). Inland capture fisheries of India has an important place, it contributes to about 30% of the total fish production. Inland capture fisheries is a continually expanding industry bringing under its fold newer fisheries of a local or regional nature, while improving upon those which are existing already.

According to Piska and Naik (2006), there are a total of about 21,585 existing species of fishes, out of which 41.2% inhabit the freshwater and the remaining marine water. India ranks seventh position among the fish producing countries of the world. China constitutes 40% of the fin fish and shell fish production, whereas India accounts for about 38% of the total fish production. Top seven fish producing countries of the world along with their production in million tones (mts) are: China (15), Japan (8.46), Peru (6.84), Chile (6.50), Russia (5.61), America (5.6) and India (4.17). India witnessed rapid growth in the fisheries sector with an increase in fish production from 2.876 million mts in 1984-85 to 4.949 million mts in 1995-96 achieving an approximate average annual growth rate of 5.4%. The sector employs about 5.96 million fishermen and supports a large workforce engaged in fisheries related ancillary activities. The export of fish and fish products was to the tune of US $1 billion mark during 1994-95.

Among the portunid crabs, *Scylla* species that are found throughout the Indo-Pacific region have become increasingly popular because of their large size and meat quality. These species are commonly found in shallow coastal waters, lagoons, brackish water lakes, estuaries, intertidal swamp and mangrove areas. With its 8,060 km long coastline, India offers a vast near shore water resources apart from the 1.7 million ha of brackish water in the adjoining coastal zone (Marichamy and Rajapackiam, 2001). Rao *et al*. (1973) estimated the potential resources of crabs from estuaries and backwaters and observed that southern coasts are richer than those of northern India.

The present study has been taken up in the coastal area of Srikakulam District. The main aim of the study was to elevate and focus the potentiality of the fishery diversity in this district which did not get any identification to the levels of the research and the work reported on the fishery of this district is meager. For this, 20 fishery landing stations of this district were selected and diversity of the fishery was analyzed to expose both fin and shell fish resources. The importance of any area will be decided on the presence of the natural resources in and around it. Due to the presence of these natural resources only, the geographical area will be popularized. But even though this district is having a long coastal belt and highly potential fishery landings through out the year, it was not explored to that extent, due to lack of proper research. So the present study was launched to elevate the fishery diversity, from 20 major fishery landing stations in Srikakulam District (Table 2.1).

Table 2.1: The diversity of fishery resources of both fin and shell fish of commercial importance is as follows from these 20 landing stations of Srikakulam District

	MOLLUSCS (Cephalopods)	
FAMILY Sepiidae (Cuttle fishes)	*Sepia pharaonis* (Ehrenberg, 1831)	Charla kalivinda
	Sepiella inermis (Fereussac & Orbigny, 1848)	Budda kalivinda
FAMILY Loliginidae (Squids)	*Loligo duvauceli* (d'Orbigny, 1848)	Kaliminda
	Doryteuthis singhalensis (Ortmann, 1891)	Peda sola Kaliminda
	CRUSTACEANS	
FAMILY Penaeidae (Penaeid shrimps)	*Penaeus monodon* (Fabricus, 1798)	Royya
	Penaeus indicus (H.Milne Edwards, 1837)	Tella royya
	Penaeus japonicus (Bata, 1888)	Pappu royya
	Metapenaeus affinis (H.Milne Edwards, 1837)	Gulla royya
	Metapenaeus brevicornis (H. Milne Edwards, 1837)	Pasupu royya
FAMILY Palinuridae (Spiny lobsters)	*Panulirus polyphagus* (Herbest, 1793)	Aaroyya
	Panulirus homarus (Linnaeus, 1758)	Rathi royya
FAMILY Scyllaridae (Slipper lobsters)	*Thenus orientalis* (Lund, 1793)	Meesala royya
FAMILY Portunidae (Crabs)	*Scylla serrata* (Forskal, 1775)	Mandapeetha
	Scylla tranquebarica (Fabricius, 1798)	Mandapeetaha/Budagottupetha
	Portunus pelagicus (Linnaeus, 1766)	Salipetha
	Portunus sangunolentus (Herbst, 1783)	Chukka petha
	Charybdis feriatus (Linnaeus, 1758)	Yerra petha

(Contd...)

Elasmobranches: (Cartilaginous Fishes)

FAMILY	SCIENTIFIC NAME	VERNACULAR NAME
Rhiniodontidae (Whale Shark)	*Rhiniodon typus* (Smith, 1828)	Guna sorra
Odontaspididae (Sand sharks)	*Eugomphodus taurus* (Rafinesque, 1810)	Tella sorra
Carcharhinidae (Requiem Sharks)	*Carcharhinus brevipinna* (Muller and Henle, 1839)	Sorra
	Carcharhinus limbatus (Valenciennes, in Muller & Henle, 1839)	Sorra
	Carcharhinus melanopterus (Quoy and Gaimard, 1824)	Commu sorra
	Galeocerdo arcticus (Faber, 1829)	Boba sorra
	Rhizoprionodon acutus (Ruppell 1837)	Matchala sorra
	Rhizoprionodon ologolinx (Springer 1964)	Sem sorra
	Scoliodon laticaudus (Muller and Henle, 1838)	Kitalam sorra
Sphyrnidae (Hammerhead-Sharks)	*Eusphyra blochii* (Cuvier, 1817)	Kommu sorra
	Sphyrna zygaena (Linnaeus, 1758)	Kommu sorra
Dasyatidae (String/Whip Rays)	*Dasyatis bleekeri* (Blyth, 1860)	Mullu teeki
	Dasyatis uarnak (Forskal, 1775)	Garuku teeki
	Dasyatis zugei (Muller and Henle, 1841)	Teeki
	Gymnura poecilura (Shaw, 1804)	Teeki cunsul

(Contd...)

Myliobatidae (Cow-nosed Rays)	*Aetobatus narinari* (Euphrasen, 1790)	Chukka teeki
	Aetomylaeus nichofii (Bloch and Schneider, 1801)	Mokara teeki
Rhinopteridae (Cow-nosed Rays)	*Mobula diabolus* (Shaw, 1804)	Deyyam teeki
	TELEOSTS (Bony fishes)	
FAMILY	SCIENTIFIC NAME	VERNACULAR NAME
Clupeidae	*Anodontostoma chacunda* (Hamilton – Buchanan, 1822)	Madurulla
Sub-family: Dussumieriinae	*Dussumieria acuta* (Valenciennes, 1847)	Morrava
Sub-family: Clupeinae (Sardines)	*Escualosa thoracata* (Valenciennes, 1847)	Kavallu
	Sardinella albella (Valenciennes, 1847)	Kavallu
	Sardinella longiceps (Valenciennes, 1847)	Nooni kavallu
	Sardinella fimbriata (Valenciennes, 1847)	Mulla kavallu
	Sardinella gibbosa (Bleeker, 1849)	Soodimuthi
Sub-family: Pristigasterinae	*Ilisha megaloptera* (Swainson, 1839)	Ilasa
	Ilisha melastoma (Schneider, 1801)	Enagallu
	Opisthopterus tardoore (Cuvier, 1829)	Tardoore
	Pellona ditchela (Valenciennes, 1847)	Morava
Sub-family: Alosinae	Tenualosa toil (Valenciennes, 1847)	Keeli ilasa

(Contd…)

FAMILY Engraulidae (Anchovies)	*Coilia dussumieri* (Valenciennes, 1848)	Pasupupara
	Stolephorus commersoni (lacepede, 1803)	Nethallu
	Stolephorus devisi (Whitley, 1940)	Namala Nethallu
	Stolephorus indicus (Van Hasselt, 1823)	Nethallu
	Stolephorus waitei (Jordan & Seale, 1926)	Poorava
	Thryssa dussumieri (Valenciennes, 1848)	Potti porava
	Thryssa malabarica (Bloch, 1795)	Porava
	Thryssa mystax (Schneider, 1801)	Porava
	Thryssa setirostris (Broussonet, 1782)	Yeeka Porava
FAMILY Chirocentridae (Wolf herrings)	*Chirocentrus dorab* (Forskal, 1775)	Mullu vala
	Chirocentrus nudus (Swainson, 1839)	Vala
FAMILY Megalopidae (Tarpons)	*Megalops cyprinoides* (Broussonet, 1782)	Karrianga
FAMILY Congridae (Conger Eels)	*Uroconger lepturus* (Richardson, 1848)	Nalla pamu
FAMILY Muraenesocidae (Pike Congers)	*Congrssox talabonoides* (Bleeker, 1853)	Tella pamu
	Muraenesox cinereus (Forskal, 1775)	Pasupu pamu
FAMILY Chanidae (Milkfish)	*Chanos chanos* (Forskal, 1775)	Pala bontha

(Contd...)

FAMILY Ariidae (Catfishes)	*Arius arius* (Hamilton, 1822)	Jella
	Arius dussumieri (Valenciennes, 1840)	Kadi jella
	Arius jella (Day, 1877)	Mukku jella
	Arius sona (Hamilton, 1822)	Sunku jella
	Arius tenuispinis (Day, 1877)	Nalla jella
	Arius thalassinus (Ruppell, 1837)	Tella jella
FAMILY Plotosidae (Catfisj eels)	*Plotosus canius* (Hamilton-Buchanan, 1822)	Engali
FAMILY Synodidae (Lizard fishes)	*Saurida tumbil* (Bloch, 1795)	Bade matta
	Saurida undosquamis (Richardson, 1848)	Bade matta
FAMILY Harpadontidae (Bombay-duck)	*Harpadon nehereus* (Hamilton – Buchanan, 1822)	Vana matta
FAMILY Bregmaceros maclellandi	*Bregmaceros maclellandi* (Thompson, 1840)	Bontha
FAMILY Hemiramphidae (Hakf-beaks)	*Hemiramphus lutkei* (Valenciennes, 1846)	Muddera
	Hyporhamphus dussumieri (Valenciennes, 1846)	Kolasa
	Rhynchorhamphus malabaricus (Valenciennes, 1846)	Muduru kolasa
FAMILY Belonidae (Needlefishes)	*Strongylura strongylura* (Van Hassett, 1823)	Potti pichika
	Tylosurus raphidoma (Ranzain, 1842)	Kaduru

(Contd...)

FAMILY Platycephalidae (Flat-heads)	*Grammoplites scaber* (Linnaeus, 1758)	Errawa
FAMILY Centropomidae (Sea-perches)	*Lates calcarifer* (Bloch, 1790)	Pandu goppa
FAMILY Ambassidae (Glassy perchlets)	*Ambassis gymnocephalus* (Lacepede, 1801)	Sudumulu
FAMILY Serranidae (Sea-Basses)	*Cephalopholis boenack* (Bloch, 1790) *Cephalopholis sonnerati* (Valenciennes, 1828) *Epinephelus areolatus* (Forskal, 1775) *Epinephelus malabaricus* (Schneider, 1801) *Epinephelus tauvina* (Forskal, 1775) *Promicrops lanceolatus* (Bloch,1790)	Bonthu Bonthu Rathi bohthu Kodi punju Maru bonthu Bonthu
FAMILY Teraponidae (Terapons)	*Terapon jarbua* (Forsakl, 1775) *Terapon puta* (Cuvier, 1829) *Terapon theraps* (Cuvier, 1829)	Keeli pothu Potti keeli Keelothu
FAMILY Priacanthidae (Big-eyes)	*Priacanthus boops* (Bloch & Schneider, 1801) *Priacanthus hamrur* (Forskal, 1775) *Priacanthus tayenus* (Richardson, 1846) *Priacanthus cruentatus* (Lacepede, 1802)	Bocchu Yerra-chepa Bocchu Yerrabocchu
FAMILY Sillaginidae (Sillagos)	*Sillaginopsis panijus* (Hamilton-Buchanan, 1822) *Sillago sihama* (Forskal, 1775)	Yeerra soringi Soringi

(Contd…)

FAMILY Lactariidae (Whitefish)	*Lactarius lactarius* (Bloch & Schneider, 1801)	Chudumu
FAMILY Rachycentridae	*Rachycentron canadum* (Linnaeus, 1766)	Nalla matta
FAMILY Carangidae	*Alectis indicus* (Ruppell, 1830)	Gundupara
	Alepes djedaba (Forskal, 1775)	Kara
	Caranx para (Cuvier, 1833)	Sudumukara
	Carangoides malabaricus (Bloch and Schneider)	Para
	Caranx carangus (Bloch, 1793)	Pasupu para
	Caranx ignobilis (Forskal, 1775)	Pasupu para
	Caranx sexfasciatis (Quoy & Gaimard, 1824)	Chukka para
	Decapterus russelli (Ruppell, 1830)	Wadagawa
	Gnathanodon speciosus (Forskal, 1775)	Gundu para
	Megalapsis cordyla (Linnaeus, 1758)	Kaduru
	Scomberoides commersonianus (Lacepede, 1802)	Tholu para
	Selar crumenophthalmus (Bloch, 1793)	Betti parigi
	Trachinotus blochii (lacepede, 1801)	Chandamama para
	Formio niger (Bloch & Schneider, 1801)	Nalla sandava
FAMILY Coryphaenidae (Dolphinfishes)	*Coryphaena hippurus* (Linnaeus, 1758)	Peda kara

(*Contd...*)

FAMILY Menidae (Moonfishes)	*Mene maculata* (Bloch & Schneider, 1801)	Mangali kitti
FAMILY Leiognathidae (Ponyfishes)	*Leiognathus bindus* (Valenciennes, 1835) *Leiognathus equulus* (Forskal, 1775) *Secutor insidiator* (Bloch, 1787) *Secutor ruconius* (Hamilton – Buchanan, 1822)	Bandu kara Chanduva kara Chukka kara Chinna Chukkakara
FAMILY Lutjanidae (Jobfishes)	*Lutjanus argentimaculatus* (Forskal, 1775) *Lutjanus johni* (Bloch, 1792)	Verra kachidi Rangu
FAMILY Lobotidae (Triple tails)	*Lobotes surinamensis* (Bloch, 1790)	Maata
FAMILY Haemulidae (Pomadasidae)	*Pomadasys maculates* (Bloch, 1797)	Caripe
FAMILY Lethrinidae (Emperors)	*Lethrinus fraenatus* (Valenciennes, 1830)	Karwa
FAMILY Sparidae (Seabreams)	*Argyrops spinifer* (Forskal, 1775) *Rhabdosargus sarba* (Forskal, 1775)	Yerra goraka Chittichelee

(Contd...)

FAMILY Sciaenidae (Jew fishes)	*Atrobucca nide* (Jordan & Thompson, 1911)	Karrimuthi goraka
	Johnius macropterus (Beeker, 1853)	Gorasa
	Johnieops sina (Cuvier, 1830)	Nalla goraka
	Kathala axillaris (Cuvier, 1830)	Palli goraka
	Nibea maculate (Schneider, 1801)	Nalla Machala goraka
	Otolithoides biauritus (Cantor, 1850)	Goraka
	Otolithes cuvieri (Trewavas, 1976)	Panna
	Otolithes ruber (Schneider, 1801)	Pala goraka
	Pennahia macrophalmus (Bleeker, 1850)	Gorasa
	Protonibea diacanthus (Lecepede, 1802)	Chukkala gorasa
FAMILY Mullidae (Goatfishes)	*Parupeneus indicus* (Shaw, 1803)	Rathi gulivinda
	Upeneus sulphureus (Cuvier, 1829)	Goolivinda
	Upeneus vittatus (Forskal, 1775)	Erra gulivuinda
FAMILY) Monodactylidae (Bat fishes	*Monodactylus argenteus* (Linnaeus, 1758)	Chandamamapara
FAMILY Ephippidae (Spadefishes)	*Drepane punctata* (Linnaeus, 1758)	Tharalam
Sub-Family Ephippinae	*Ephippus orbid* (Bloch, 1787)	Pasupu goraka
FAMILY Scatophagidae	*Scatophagus argus* (Bloch, 1788)	Errava

(Contd...)

FAMILY Pomacanthidae (Anglefishes)	*Pomacanthus annularis* (Bloch, 1787)	Parigi
FAMILY Mugilidae (Mullets)	*Liza parsia* (Hamilton-Buchanan, 1822) *Liza tade* (Forskal, 1775) *Liza vaigiensis* (Quoy & Gaimard, 1824) *Mugil cephalus* (Linnaeus, 1758)	Bontha Kanisi Pitta parigi Pitta parigi
FAMILY Sphyraenidae (Barracudas)	*Sphyraena obtusata* (Cuvier, 1829) *Sphyraena jello* (Cuvier, 1829)	Seela vothu Seelabothu
FAMILY Polynemidae (Threadfins)	*Eleuthronema tetradactulum* (Shaw, 1804) *Polynemus heptadactylus* (Cuvier, 1829) *Polynemus indicus* (Shaw,1804)	Maga Boddu maga Maga
FAMILY Acanthuridae	*Acanthurus tristegus* (Linnaeus 1758)	Mootah
FAMILY Siganidae (Rabbit fishes)	*Siganus canaliculatus* (Park, 1797)	Warawah
FAMILY Trichiuridae (Ribbon fishes)	*Eupleurogrammus glossodon* (Bleeker, 1860) *Lepturacanthus savala* (Cuvier, 1829) *Trichiyrus lepturus* (Linnaeus, 1758)	Savada Savada Nalla Savada

(Contd...)

FAMILY Scombridae (Tunas)	*Auxis thazard* (Laccepede, 1800) *Euthynnus affinis* (Cantor, 1849) *Katsuwonus pelamis* (Linnaeus, 1758) *Scomberomorus commerson* (Lecepede, 1801) *Scomberomorus lineolatus* (Cuvier, 1831) *Thunnus albacares* (Bonnaterre, 1788) *Rastrelliger kanagurta* (Cuvier, 1817)	Sura Chukka Sura Gedu sura Konava Vanjaram Pasupu sura Kanagaratha
FAMILY Xiphidae (Swordfishes)	*Xiphias gladius* (Linnaeus, 1758)	Kommukonava
FAMILY Istiophoridae	*Istiophorus platypterus* (Shawand Nodder, 1792) *Makaira indica* (Cuvier, 1832)	Nemalipuri konava Nalla kommukonava
FAMILY Ariommidae	*Arimma indica* (Day, 1870)	Mettapara
FAMILY Stromateidae (Pomfrets)	*Pampus argenteus* (Euphrasen, 1788) *Pampus chinensis* (Euphrasen, 1788)	Tella sanduva Nalla Sanduva
FAMILY Bothidae (Left eye flounders)	*Pseudorhombus arsius* (Hamilton, 1822)	Namminalika
FAMILY Soleidae (Soles)	*Synaptura commersoniana* (Lacepede, 1802)	Kitalam para

FUTURE PROSPECTS AND CONCLUSIONS

Srikakulam District is having a long coastal area with more potential fishery landing stations. But the resources are still remained unexplored and so far there are no reports from this area. The fishery in this district is seen all around the year, which is done by operating different traditional and mechanized craft and gear. The most important thing to be noticed here is there is no specific harvest period followed by the fisher men in this entire coast. As a result, there is no regulation in the catches and mostly the juveniles and the berried ones are caught and the landings are being declined gradually. So the state government has to take proper action to regulate this condition.

The fishery landing stations with more landings are Bandaruvanipeta, Rajaramapuram, Mogadharapadu, Srikurmam-matschyalesam, Kunduvanipeta and Kallepalli.

The landing stations with more diversity of fishes are Bandaruvanipeta, Mogadharapadu and Kallepalli.

REFERECCES

Ayyappan, S and Jena, J.K. (2003). Indian Fisheries and Aquaculture: Present and Future Prospects. In: *Fish for All,* National launch, Kolkata. pp. 12-24.

Marichamy, M and Rajapackiam . S (2001). The Aquaculture of *Scylla* Species in India. *Proceedings of the International Forum on the Culture of Portunid Crabs. Asian Fisheries Science* 14, pp. 231-238.

Pillai, N.G.K. and Pradeep, K. Katiha (2004). *Evolution of Fisheries and Aquaculture in India,* p 240. Central Marine Fisheries Research Institute, Kochi-18, India.

Piska.R.S and Naik. S.J.K.(2006) *Brakishwater and Marine Fisheries.*

Rao, P. Vedavyasa, M.M. Thomas and G. Sudhakara Rao. 1973. The Crab Fishery Resources of India. *Proceedings of Symposium on Living Resources of the Seas around India.* pp. 581-591.

3

Fish Diversity of Noyyal River Basin, Coimbatore Tamil Nadu

V. Maruthappan[1]
M. Ramesh[1]

ABSTRACT

This study examined the physical and chemical properties of waters of Noyyal river basin, Coimbatore, Tamil Nadu for period of 12 months (2007). The implications on the public health and fish diversity were also determined. River was sampled at middle zone of the river and mixing of the municipal sewage with river. Standard methods were used to monitor the physical and chemical parameters. Physical parameters that were considered include; temperature, colour, total suspended solid and turbidity. The chemical parameters include hardness, chemical oxygen demand (COD), biological oxygen demand (BOD), dissolved oxygen (DO), pH, chlorides, phosphates,

Unit of Toxicology, Department of Zoology, Bharathiar University, Coimbatore – 641 046, *E.mail:* zoomaruthu@yahoo.co.in

carbonates and bicarbonates. Seasonal variation appeared to have influence on the physical and chemical parameters. Statistical analysis shows that there were significant differences between sampling points and different locations mean values for the different physical and chemical parameters examined. The presence of fish diversity affected some parameters such as BOD, DO, COD, pH and turbidity significantly. The BOD & COD were strongly significant correlated and positively correlated ($r=0.757$, $P \leq 0.05$).

Key words: Water quality, Middle zone, Sewage mixing zone, Physicochemical parameters.

INTRODUCTION

The Noyyal river is a tributary of the Cauvery, a large interstate river which cuts through the States of Karnataka and Tamilnadu and enters the Bay of Bengal. The Noyyal flows through the districts of Coimbatore, Erode and Karur and the urban centers of Coimbatore and Tiruppur, in western Tamil Nadu (see Fig. 3.1). A number of industrial units such as textile units, chemicals, and electroplating are located in the river basin which discharges their untreated and partially treated effluents into the river. In addition, sewage from Coimbatore and Tiruppur cities is also being discharged into the river without much treatment, making the Noyyal one of the highly polluted rivers in the country.

The Noyyal is a seasonal river which has good flow only for short periods during the North-East and South-West monsoons. Occasionally flash floods occur when there is heavy rain in the catchment areas. Apart from these periods, there is only scanty flow for most parts of the year. The river supplies water to several irrigation tanks located in and around Coimbatore town and downstream. Nearly 6,000 acres of cultivable land in Coimbatore district are irrigated using the river water.

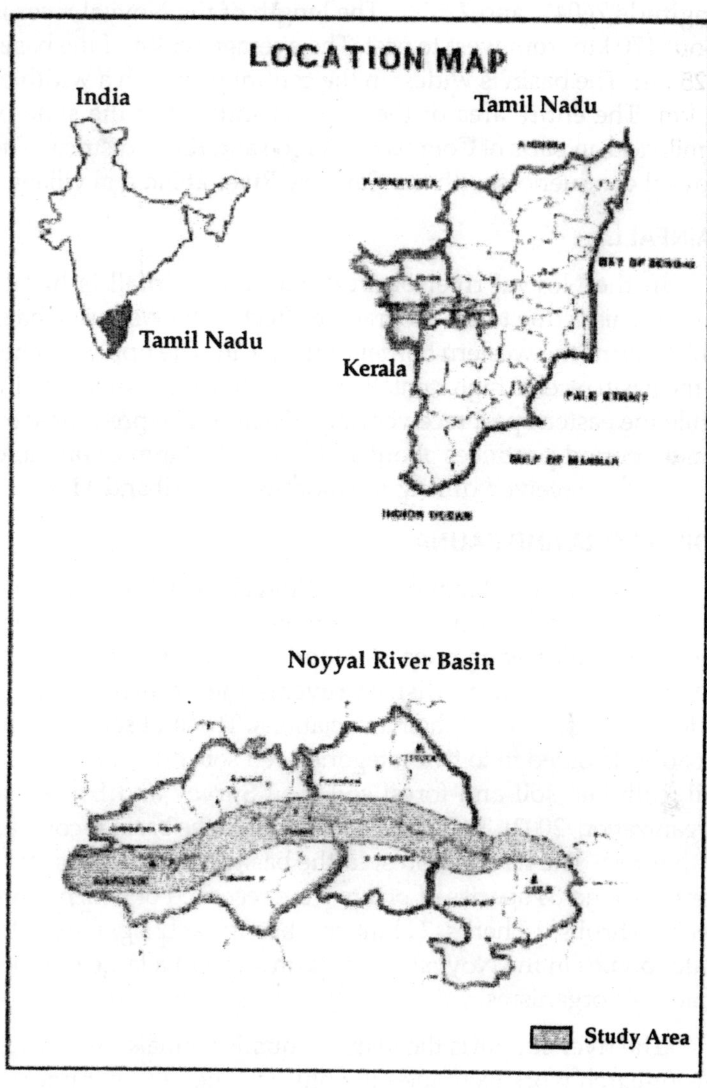

Fig. 3.1 The study area of Noyyal River

The Noyyal river basin covers a total area of 3510 km^2 and is located between north latitude 10056′ and 11019′ and east longitude 76041′ and 77056′. The length of the Noyyal river is about 170 km from west to east. The average width of the basin is 25 km. The basin is widest in the central part with a width of 35 km. The entire area of the basin is situated in the state of Tamilnadu, in parts of Coimbatore, Erode and Karur districts. The Noyyal confluences with the Cauvery River at Noyyal village.

RAINFALL

In the Noyyal river basin the annual rainfall is highly varied. This is due to the orographic effect of the Western Ghats, which forms the western border of the basin. The upper reaches of the basin receive high rainfall of more than 3000 mm annually, while the eastern part receives only 600 mm. The pre-monsoon season period produces about 100 mm to 300 mm of rain and most of it is received during the months of April and May.

SOIL, FLORA AND FAUNA

The type of soil that occur in Noyyal basin are many and varied, ranging from shallow red non-calcareous soils to very deep grey calcareous ones. A standard reconnaissance soils survey of Coimbatore district reveals the occurrence of 14 different soil series and their associations. These 14 series can be broadly classified in to five categories: red soil, grey soil, alluvial soil, colluvial soil and forest soil (Soil Survey and Land Use Organization, 2002). The upper catchment of the basin is covered with forest. The natural forest in the basin consists of verity of flora. Around 34 species of plants were recorded of which: 3 are trees, 8 shrubs, 17 herbs, 3 climbers, 1 sedge and 2 grasses. The water bodies in the Noyyal River Basin support a large number of aquatic organisms.

The river supports the lives of aquatic animals. As a result this research work examined the physico-chemical parameters of these waters. Information provided in this study will assist in the better management of water resources in the river. Communities that use untreated supplies such as most villages in the developing countries face more serious problems, if there is a chemical problem associated with their water sources. If they lack a necessary chemical it will be extremely difficult to add some chemical and since the water is untreated, it is impossible to removed harmful chemical pollutants. In addition chemical water pollution may leads to an unpleasant taste or appearance and this may cause people to abandon certain sources in favour of other which are more acceptable to them. Water chemistry may be considered under three headings:

(i) The essence of necessary chemical;

(ii) The excess of harmful organics;

(iii) The excess of harmful inorganics (Sandy & Richard, 1995).

The modern society or communities are concerned about the quality of their water resources and are confronted by a number of problems threatening these resources. One obstacle in accessing the magnitude of this problem is difficulty of defining acceptable water quality for specific uses. It is defined that water quality as any characteristics of water, whether physical, chemical and biological, that affects the survival, reproduction, growth and management of fish. However more stringent control of water contaminants and higher quality standards apply to water intended for human consumption than for other uses.

MATERIALS AND METHODS

Sampling and Analysis

Two sampling points were sited for Noyyal river. They are middle zone of the river and mixing of the municipal sewage with river. Sampling depth was 20 cm. River was sampled for 12 months (from January to December 2007). Sampling bottles of 1 liter capacity were used. A total of 150 water samples were collected and analyses to understand the impact of water quality. Samples were taken in triplicates and average figures were recorded. Samples were analysed for physical and chemical parameters. These include temperature, colour, total suspended solid and turbidity, hardness, chemical oxygen demand (COD), biological oxygen demand (BOD), dissolved oxygen (DO), pH, chlorides, phosphates, carbonates and bicarbonates according to methods described APHA (1998). Pearson correlation co-efficient and student's't' test were used for statistical analysis.

The fish collection was done for a period of four months interval. The fish collection was done with the help of different type of gill net with different mesh sizes. After collection, fishes were examined; numbers were counted and released to the system. Few specimens (2-5) were preserved at 10% formalin for further laboratory studies. In the laboratory, the fishes were identified based on the morphometric and meristic characters with the help of standard taxonomic text books (Jhingran, 1991; Jayaram, 1999).

RESULTS

According to Rand and Petrocelli (1985) the physicochemical parameters of the water may influence the toxicity of toxicant present in the water, which may affect the fishes or the distribution of the fishes. In the present study the Noyyal river basin was studied to know the impact of aquatic pollution on fish diversity.

Table 3.1 shows the mean values of the physi-cochemical characteristics of the Noyyal river basin, Coimbatore, Tamil Nadu during the year 2007. In 2007 (from January to December) the physicochemical variations were examined according to the sampling zones are as follows: the colour, temperature, pH, biological oxygen demand (BOD, chemical oxygen demand (COD), dissolved oxygen (DO), dissolved free CO_2, total hardness, chlorides, phosphate, carbonate, bicarbonate, turbidity and total suspended solids across various sampling zones were statistically and significantly varying ($P \leq 0.05$).

Table 3.1: Mean values of the physico-chemical characteristics of the Noyyal river basin, Coimbatore, Tamilnadu during the year 2007

Sl. No.	*Parameters*	*Mean Values ± Std. Deviation*	
		Sample from middle zone of the pond	*Sample from sewage mixing zone of the pond*
1.	Colour	Pale green	Pale green
2.	Temperature (°C)	26.00±1.00	27.20±1.20
3.	pH	7.90±1.00	6.20±0.80
4.	COD (mg/l)	8.12±1.39	8.90±1.20
5.	BOD (mg/l)	11.02±1.92	12.00±0.50
6.	Dissolved Oxygen (mg/l)	4.12±0.25	3.73±0.90
7.	Dissolved free CO_2 (mg/l)	15.00±0.20	17.00±0.22
8.	Total Hardness (mg/l)	30.00±0.80	48.70±0.91
9.	Chlorides (ppm)	350±0.40	500±0.50
10.	Phosphates (ppm)	0.60±0.01	0.12±0.05
11.	Carbonates (ppm)	0.0014±0.05	0.0025±0.01
12.	Bicarbonates (ppm)	0.060±0.04	0.150±0.03
13.	Turbidity (cm)	120±1.20	141±1.00
14.	Total suspended solid (mg/l)	0.01±0.20	0.13±0.50

The colour of the both middle zone and sewage mixing zone of the river was pale green. The temperature in the middle zone (mean=26.00) was statistically and significantly varying ($P \leq 0.05$) lesser than the sewage mixing zone (mean=27.20). The pH in the middle zone (mean=7.9) was statistically and significantly varying ($P \leq 0.05$) higher than the sewage mixing zone (mean=6.20). The COD in the middle zone (mean=8.12) was not statistically and significantly varying ($P \leq 0.05$) lesser than the sewage mixing zone (mean=8.96). The BOD in the middle zone (mean=11.02) was not statistically and significantly varying ($P \leq 0.05$) lesser than the sewage mixing zone (mean=12.00).

The DO of the middle zone of the river was 4.12 mg/l, whereas in the sewage mixing zone of the river it was 3.73 mg/l, which was lesser than the middle zone. The dissolved free CO_2 of the middle zone of the river was 15 mg/l, whereas in the sewage mixing zone of the river it was 17 mg/l, which was higher than the middle zone. The total hardness of the middle zone of the river was 30.00 mg/l, whereas in the sewage mixing zone of the river it was 48.7 mg/l, which was higher than the middle zone. The chloride content of the middle zone of the river was 350 mg/l, whereas in the sewage mixing zone of the river it was 500 mg/l, which was higher than the middle zone. The phosphate content of the middle zone of the river was 0.6 mg/l, whereas in the sewage mixing zone of the river it was 0.12 mg/l, which was higher than the middle zone.

The carbonate content in the middle zone (mean=0.0014) was statistically and significantly varying ($P \leq 0.05$) lesser than the sewage mixing zone (mean=0.0025). The bicarbonate content in the middle zone (mean=0.060) was statistically and significantly varying ($P \leq 0.05$) lesser than the sewage mixing zone (mean=0.150). The turbidity in the middle zone (mean=120) was statistically and significantly varying ($P \leq 0.05$) lesser than the sewage mixing zone (mean=141). The total suspended solids in the middle zone (mean=0.01) was statistically and significantly varying ($P \leq 0.05$) lesser than the sewage mixing zone (mean=0.13).

RELATIONSHIP BETWEEN COD & BOD

The COD and BOD are strongly and significantly correlated and positively correlation ($P \leq 0.05$; r=0.757).

In the present study, six species of fish were (Plate 3.4) identified in the river during the study period (Table 3.2). There are:

1. *Channa striatus*
2. *Oreochromis mossambicus*
3. *Cyprinus carpio specularis*

4. *Clarias batrachus*
5. *Catla catla*
6. *Labeo rohita*

Table 3.2: Fish diversity of Noyyal river basin, Coimbatore, Tamil Nadu during the year 2007

S. No.	*Species*	*Status*	*Middle zone (No. of fish)*	*Sewage fed zone (No. of fish)*
1.	*Channa striatus*	Rare	5	0
2.	*Oreochromis mossambicus*	Common	10	4
3.	*Cyprinus carpio specularis*	Common	8	5
4.	*Clarias batrachus*	Rare	4	3
5.	*Catla catla*	Common	12	0
6.	*Labeo rohita*	Common	6	2

Plate 3.1 Wastes near the river

Plate 3.2 Sewage mixing zone

Plate 3.3 Drainage in the river

Channa striatus

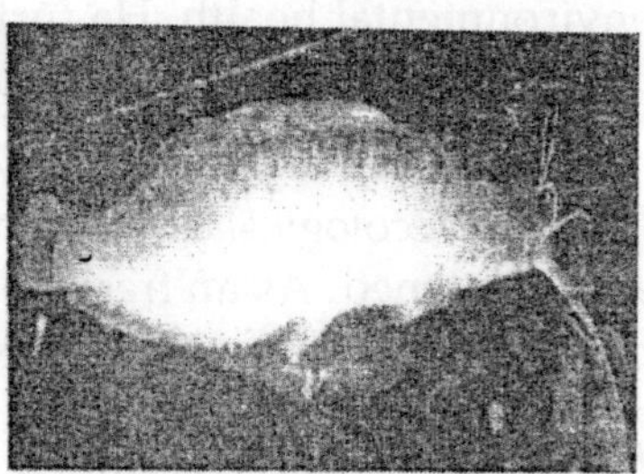
Clarias batrachus

Oreochromis mossambicus

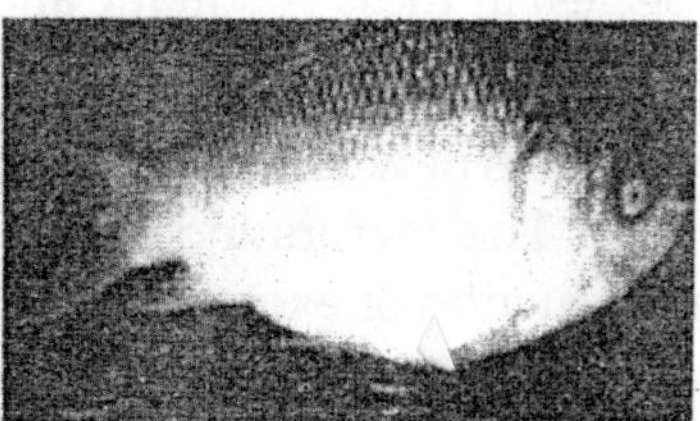
Catla catla

Cyprinus carpio specularis *Labeo rohita*

Plate 3.4 Fish species

DISCUSSION

Biodiversity is a public policy as well as a scientific issue and will be increasingly affecting all of us involved with biological resources management (Cairns and Lackey, 1992). According to Ramanathan (1964) the aquatic biodiversity has enormous economic and aesthetic value and is largely responsible for maintaining and supporting overall environmental health. He further reported that humans have long depended on aquatic resources, such as fishing and tourism.

India has high geographical diversity and this is reflected in its high ecological diversity most of Asia's freshwater habitats are threatened. Asian freshwater biodiversity in exceptionally high and contains fiver of the world's 10 countries that have the richest freshwater fish fauna. The zoological survey of India (Anonymous, 1991) recently published a status report of India's faunal wealth. According to the figures presented in the report, about 16,500 species or more than 20% of the total faunal (78,000 species) in India is aquatic and majority of this is freshwater.

Aquatic ecosystems are exposed to all local disturbances regardless of where they occur (Sugunan, 1995; Suryanarayanan, 1996). The factors includes over-exploitation of species, the introduction of exotic species, pollution from urban, industrial and agricultural areas, as well as habitat loss and alteration through damming and water diversion which contribute to the declining levels of aquatic biodiversity in both freshwater and marine environments. All over the world fish biodiversity is showing signs of decline (McNeely, 1988).

Pollution, which gives the double effect of eutrophication and intoxication, in the specific result of human activity. Some increase in eutrophication increases productivity, but its further increase usually reduces diversity intoxication reduces diversity and has no analogous factor in the natural environment further more pollution causes teratogenicity, carcinogenicity and mutagenicity in populations (Naiman *et al.*, 1988).

Brij Gopal (1997) reported that the major source of aquatic pollution in freshwater system is domestic and industrial organic wasters, although toxic metals are also a concern in some areas. Paper pulp mills and food processing plants are the main industries causing organic pollution. Disposal of domestic and industrial effluent in water bodies is one of the most serious threads to biodiversity (Patel *et al.*, 1983). Use of chemical fertilizer and pesticides by the cultivars along the rivers also degrade the habitat of dolphin. Chemical pollution, including acid rain and the excessive use of agricultural chemicals is another factor, leading to loss of fish diversity.

The pH 7.9 in the middle zone and 6.2 in the sewage mixing zone in the present investigation will also influence the toxicity of metal ions, if present in the water. The low DO level in both the zone may be due to presence of organic matter, biological activities or decay or vegetation. The high level of total hardness in both the zones may be due to weathering of rocks during which minute fragments are carried out and settle in the lake.

In the present study, a high CO_2 level was noted in both the zones. This may be due to love DO level which is toxic to fishes (Ramesh *et al.*, 1993). Similarly high level of total hardness in both the zones indicate the discharge of waste from the near by industries or sewage from near by houses.

Ellis (1973) observed that high BOD and COD levels in the effluent might reduce the DO levels in the receiving water, leading to conversion of sulphate to sulphite, which is toxic to fishes. The low DO may cause mortality of aquatic organisms. According to James and Lee (1979), the minimum DO level of fish is 7 mg/l, when DO content of water goes below critical level, mortality of fish may occur (Brain *et al.*, 1974).

Of all the nutrients, the chloride value was found to be maximum, in the present study. This may be due to the washing down of organic matter form the surrounding catchments as suggested by Dehadrai and Poniah (1997). However, the phosphates, carbonates, bicarbonates turbidity and total suspended solid level was maximum, which supports the animal, and plant life which indicate the absence of rain water during the study period. In the present study, the physicochemical parameter of the water body shows abnormal values indicating the pollution level of the river.

There is an extensive body of scientific literature on diversity, diversity indices and the structural and functional stability associated with aquatic ecosystem diversity (Hughes and

Noss, 1992). However, the convention on biological diversity adopted at the Rio Earth Summit in June 1992, has led to a resurgence of interest in the subject of biodiversity and its various human dimensions. In the present study totally six species of fish were identified. But earlier reports that more number of fish species in Noyyal river. The stocking rate of seeds in the lake was also minimum when compare to earlier reports. The decline number of species, number of species and stocking rate may be high level of pollution in the river.

Some have argued that biodiversity must be preserved regardless of any present or future materials values to human kind because of species inherent right to exist (Ehrefeld, 1978). Legislation, such as the federal water pollution control Act of 1948, indicated that degradation of water resources has long been recognized as a serious problem. However, until recently the loss of diversity in aquatic ecosystem has received relatively little attention, despite the fact that fish are the oldest, the most diverse and the largest group of vertebrates, they outnumber all other vertebrate species combined (Cairns and Lackey, 1992).

Whereas considerable attention is being paid to the decline in the diversity of fishes, avifauna and a few other vertebrates, as well as to their conservation, the importance of the diversity of planktonic and benthic organisms and aquatic vegetation is generally overlooked. It is these groups of aquatic biota, which are conical to the sustenance of fisheries and all other animals in the aquatic systems.

Numerous seminars and workshops have concentrated on the biodiversity in terrestrial ecosystems, its conservation in protected areas such as national parks and sanctuaries and its socio economic dimensions whereas the biodiversity in aquatic ecosystems, especially the freshwater where the life first originated remains neglected. Moreover, human impact has now become a future factor, which modifies the spatial structure of the fish community, for example by marked changed in the flow regime and the water quality.

CONCLUSION

In the present study it is concluded that the Noyyal river basin is highly polluted due to sewage from residential area, effluents from the industries and agriculture wastes. This leads to loss of many aquatic organisms particularly fishes. Hence both Government and public come forward to take urgent steps to ensure that the river is not regarded further by anthropogenic activities.

REFERENCES

APHA, AWWA AND WPCF, 1998. *In*: 'Standard Methods for the Examination of Water and Waste Water'. *American Public Wealth Association*, Washington, USA, 874.

Anonymous, 1991. *Animal Resources of India: Protozoa to Mammalia. State of the Art*, Zoological Survey of India, Calcutta, p. 694.

Brain, J.L., Berry, Rank, and Horton, E., 1974. *Urban Environment Management Planning for Pollution Control*, Prentice Hall Inc., Englewood cliffs, New Jersey.

Cairns, M.A. and Lackey, R.T., 1992. Biodiversity and Management of Natural Resources: *Fish*, 17(3): 6-10.

Dehadrai, P.V. and Poniah, A.G., 1997. Conserving Indian's Fish Biodiversity, *Inter. J. Environ. Sci.* 23: 305-313. International Scientific Publications, New Delhi.

Ehrenfeld, D., 1978. *The Arrogance of Humanism.* Oxford University Press, New York.

Ellis, A.E., 1973. The Leucocytes of Fish: A Review, *J. Fish, 11*: 453-491.

Brij Gopal, B., 1997. Biodiversity in Inland Aquatic Ecosystems in India an Overview. *International J. Ecol. Environ. Sci., 23*: 305-313.

Hughes, R.M. and Noss, R., 1922. Biological Diversity and Biological Integrity: Current Concerns for Lakes and Streams. *Fish.*, (Bethesda) 17(3): 11.

James, A.E., 1979. *Water Resources and Environmental Engineering.* McGraw Hill Book Company.

Jayaram, K.C., 1999. *The Freshwater Fishes of India.* Zoological Survey of India, Calcutta.

Jhingran, A.G., 1991. Challenging Frontiers is Freshwater Fisheries of India. *In*: Aquatic Sciences in India. (Eds.) *South Asian Publishing Company*, New Delhi, pp. 31-49.

McNeely, J.A., 1988. *Economics and Biological Diversity*, International Union for Conservation of National Resources, Gland Switzerland.

Naiman, R.J., Decamps, H., Pastor, J. and Johnson, C.A., 1988. The Potential Importance of Boundaries of Fluvial Ecosystem. *J. North Amer. Benthol Soc.*, 7: 289-306.

Patel, S.G., Singh, D.D. and Harshly, D.K., 1983. Pamital (Jabalpur) – Sewage Polluted Water Body, as Evidenced by Chemical and Biological Indicators of Pollution. *J. Environ. Biol.* 4(2): 437-449.

PWD, 2001. *Hand Pump and Power Pump Water Quality Data for Tiruppur Block*, TWADS Board Database, Coimbatore.

Ramanathan, K.R. 1964. *Ulotrichales*. Indian Council of Agricultural Research, New Delhi.

Ramesh, M., Manavalaramanujam, R. and Sivakumari, K., 1993. Studies on the Effect of Nickel Electroporating Factory Effluent on Phosphatase Activity of Fresh Water Fish, Oreochromis Mossambicus (Peters). *Bill. Appl. Sci., 12(A)*: 41-47.

Rand, G.M. and Petrocelli, S.R., 1985. In: *Fundamental of Aquatic Toxicology Method and Applications* (Ed.) Hemisphere Publishing Corporation, Washington, USA. pp. 1-28.

Soil Survey and Land Use Organization, 2002. Ground Water Prospective: A Profile of Erode District, State Ground and Surface Water Resources Data Centre, Water Resources Organization, Chennai.

Sugunan, V.V., 1995. *Reserve Fishes of Indian*. FAO Fisheries Technical Paper 345, Food and Agriculture Organization of the United Nation, Rome, p. 423.

Suryanaryanan, N., 1996. *Environmental State of the Art of Indian Lakes/ Reservoirs*. National Lake Environmental Committee Foundation, Shelia, Japan, p. 19-34.

4

Biological Considerations in Shrimp Farming

S.K. Das[1]
S.N. Padhi[2]

ABSTRACT

Shrimp farming is expanding fast in India due to several factors. Cultivable species of shrimps and resource potential for such farming are described. Types of culture and pond dynamics in shrimp ponds are cited. Two important considerations in it are shrimp nutrition and pond environment monitoring. Nutrient requirement of shrimps such as protein, amino acids, fat, energy, carbohydrate, vitamins, minerals, binders, anti oxidants etc. are discussed. Ideal water characteristics and pond bottom features are mentioned. Aquaculture Authority guidelines should be followed in shrimp farming in India.

1 Department Fishery Biology & Resources Management, Faculty of Fishery Sciences, Chakgaria, P.O. Panchasayer, Kolkata-700 094, West Bengal.

2 Department of Zoology, KBDAV College, Nirakarpur, Khurda, Orissa.

INTRODUCTION

Aqua farming is expanding fast during recent years due to its inherent capacity to produce more aqua foods, employment generation, and for earning foreign exchange through exports. It has higher productivity per unit area compared to agriculture and animal husbandry. Aquaculture is highly remunerative due to several unique characteristics such as high productivity, high food conversion ratio, putting agricultural and animal wastes for beneficial uses, help in rural economy and added advantage of getting rich protein diet. More than half of aquaculture productions of world originate from brackish water and marine environment especially the coastal zone. Brackish water environment is an intermediate water mass where both sea water and fresh water mix with each other. Its salinity varies from 0.5 to 30 ppt and such water is suitable for farming of shrimps and euryhaline fish. Brackish water shrimp farming has emerged as the most important and lucrative one due to its increasing demands in world market. Its importance is gaining momentum due to its lion's share in export of marine products in India which accounts more than two-third by value.

TIGER SHRIMP: AN IDEAL SPECIES FOR CULTURE

The Food and Agriculture Organization of United Nations had identified 343 species of shrimps having commercial importance. Among them 110 species belong to family Penaeidae accounting about 80% of world's wild caught varieties. Several penaeid species have successfully spawned in captivity which facilitate regular supply of quality seeds in need of farmers. However, five important species were identified as suitable for aquaculture as shown in Table 4.1.

Among several cultivable shrimps, *Penaeus monodon* (Fabricius) is one of the most popular and widely cultured species due to its several unique features. These have fast growth rate, good market value, euryhaline, adaptability to variations in environmental conditions, good market value, taste, abundant seed availability, resistance to stress conditions, acceptance of artificial feeds and its conversion to flesh, short gestation period etc.

Table 4.1: Five important species which are suitable for aquaculture

Sl. No.	*Species*	*Common Name*	*Countries where cultured*
1.	*Penaeus monodon*	Tiger shrimp	India, Indonesia, Vietnam, Philippines, Taiwan, China, Bangaladesh
2.	*Penaeus chinensis*	Fleshy shrimp	China, North Korea
3.	*Penaeus vanamei*	White leg shrimp	Ecuador, Mexico, Panama, Columbia
4.	*Penaeus merguinensis*	Banana shrimp	Indonesia, Vietnam, Philippines, Thailand, China
5.	*Fenneropenaeus indicus*	White shrimp	India, Indonesia, Vietnam

Culture of tiger shrimp is a financially beneficial farm practice in coastal belt of India. It has a farming activity of about 3 to 4 months duration and thus provides quick return on investment. It makes gainful utilization of unutilized coastal swampy areas and thus generates good employment opportunities in remote coastal belt of India. The laden inshore area, backwaters, brackish water areas and estuarine zones are neither suitable for human habitation nor profitable for agricultural crops. It can be suitably and effectively used for brackish water shrimp culture to achieve the success of 'Aquaplosion'. Employment opportunities got expanded in coastal areas by shrimp farming. The average labour requirement for paddy cultivation is 180 labour-days/crop/ha versus 600 labour-days/crop/ha in shrimp farming. In former, only one crop is done in a year versus two crops per year in the latter case. The agricultural labourers on average can earn Rs. 7,500 per year versus Rs. 12,000 per annum in shrimp farming (Ravichandran, 2006).

TYPES OF SHRIMP CULTURE

There are different types of shrimp culture based on management practice involved and they are classified as follows:

Improved Traditional: It is done in tide fed ponds in traditional manner. Selective stocking and feeding with local feeds are adopted to increase production. Here, stocking density varies from 40,000 to 60,000 seeds per ha per crop.

Modified Extensive: There is not much difference between improved traditional and modified extensive farming. It can be done in either tide fed or pump fed ponds. But shrimps are fed with high protein pellet feeds in this case. Water exchange is practiced in little extent.

Semi Intensive: Here, stocking density is increased to 1 to 3 lakh seeds per ha. Water quality is monitored with regular water exchange and aeration. Feeding management is practised with use of high protein diets. Health management practice is also adopted.

Intensive: Shrimp cultured under fully controlled conditions with high stocking of 5 to 10 lakh seeds per ha. Advanced farm management practice is followed here. It is not now practiced in India due to several adverse effects.

RESOURCE POTENTIAL

India has rich potential for culture of brackish water shrimps as presented in the Table 4.2. India has a coast line of 8118 km in nine states and four union territories. Its eastern coast is low-lying with lagoons, marshes, deltas while western coast is dominated by rocky shores. Fourteen major river systems of India have led to formation of wide net work of creeks and estuaries in coastal areas and thus providing an added advantage to shrimp culture. India has rich brackish water resource comprising a total estuarine belt of 3.9 million ha, back waters of 3.5 million ha, mangroves of 0.4 million ha etc. Out of it, only 1.2 million ha is being identified as suitable for brackish water aquaculture.

Table 4.2: Area under shrimp farming in India (2003-2004)

Sl. No.	*States/UT*	*Potential Area(ha)*	*Area in culture (ha)*	*Per cent of Potential*
1.	West Bengal	405,000	50,405	12.44
2.	Orissa	31,600	12,877	40.44
3.	Andhra Pradesh	150,000	76,687	51.12
4.	Tamil Nadu	56,000	5,286	9.44
5.	Pondicherry	800	130	16.25
6.	Kerala	65,000	14,106	21.70
7.	Karnataka	8,000	1,910	23.87
8.	Goa	18,500	310	1.68
9.	Maharashtra	80,000	1,281	1.60
10.	Gujarat	376,000	2,271	0.60
	Total	1,19,900	165,263	13.88

Source: Ravichandran, 2006.

POND DYNAMICS

There occurs complex physical, chemical and biological processes in the pond environment. Study of these processes and their dynamic inter-actions is referred as pond dynamics and it depends on principles of aquatic ecology and limnology. Extensive aquaculture ponds have less capacity to produce food for fish. There is threshold standing crop in such ponds above which food resources start to become limiting and it is referred as critical standing crop (CSC). At a standing crop above CSC, there is competition for food resources, and fish/shrimp crop no longer achieve maximum growth rate. There are three ways to increase the CSC in ponds. These are:

1. stocking with different compatible species so that each species can utilize different feeding niches in the pond;
2. enhancing production of natural foods like plankton and benthos with judicious use of manures and fertilizers; and
3. supplementary feeding with quality pellet feeds.

ne primary inorganic nutrients like carbon, nitrogen and iosphorus enter the photoautotrophic pathway, whereas organic nutrients are processed through the heterotrophic (detrital) pathway or are consumed by the target species directly. The left out supplementary feed in ponds are source of organic and inorganic nutrients which can enter both autotrophic and heterotrophic food chains. Fertilisation removes nutrient limitations to autotrophic and heterotrophic processes but supplementary feeds are directly consumed by the candidate species and thus the former feed the pond while the latter feeds the the crop. In extensive systems of aquaculture, a major proportion of mass and energy flows through the autotrophic path (photosynthesis > respiration). But semi intensive systems are heterotrophic (photosynthesis < respiration) where most of shrimp nutrition comes from artificial feeds. The movement of energy and mass in any aqua farming system involves both autotrophic and heterotrophic pathways. Photoautotrophs (Photosynthesizers) consume inorganic carbon and produce oxygen. On the other hand, heterotrophs consume oxygen and organic carbon and produce carbon dioxide. So, oxygen dynamics of pond depends on the balance of autotrophic and heterotrophic production which can provide idea to manage water quality (Fast and Lannan,1992). Knowledge on pond dynamics is necessary to manipulate inputs to enhance the production in shrimp farming ponds in sustainable manner.

FARM MANAGEMENT

It is sum total of interventions designed to achieve optimum production in farming. Usually, three factors such as quality seed, quality feed and ideal pond environment are very much crucial for the purpose. It is always desirable to procure disease free PCR tested seeds from shrimp hatchery. The farmer can manipulate the feed and pond environment to enhance the yield. A brief note on shrimp nutrition and pond management is given here.

Shrimp Nutrition and Feeds

Natural feed is not adequate to enhance the CSC in modified extensive or semi intensive culture practice. So feed is the most important input to increase the production in it. An ideal feed should contain adequate amount of proteins, energy, lipids, carbohydrates, vitamins, minerals and must have good digestibility.

Proteins are used for growth and repair of tissue. Its inadequacy will cause reduction in growth and loss of weight due to withdrawal of protein from tissues to maintain the vital body functions. Excess of it is converted to energy or excreted. Protein is a costly item in the diet and its incorporation needs to be in optimum level to reduce cost of diet. Its recommended levels vary from 30% to 57% in diet depending size and species in different shrimps. It is around 40 to 45 percent in the case of tiger shrimp in culture/grow out ponds. Amino acid level in diet needs to be adequate for good growth. There are essential and non-essential amino acids. The former is either not synthesized by shrimp or synthesized at very low level that results in less than optimal growth. The latter are synthesized to the level needed for optimal growth. Essential amino acids needed for shrimp are methionone, arginine, threonine, tryptophan, histidine, isoleucine, leucine, lysine, valine and phenyle alanine.

Shrimps require relatively less dietary energy because it need not have to maintain constant body temperature and they excrete most of nitrogenous waste as ammonia than urea or uric acid where less energy is lost in protein catabolism. Lipids are fat soluble compounds like fats, phospholipids, shingomyelins, waxes and sterols. It provides energy and used as precursor for several compounds. Its level in the diet varies from 6 to 7.5 percent. Four fatty acids essential in shrimp diet are linoleic, linolenic, eicosapentaenoic and decosahexaenoic fatty acids. Phospholipids and cholesterols at levels of around 1.0 and 0.30 percent may be incorporated in the diet for good growth. Carbohydrate is least expensive item of dietary energy and its utilization in shrimp metabolism is limited. When adequate lipid or carbohydrate is available, shrimp will use protein for growth. Fiber level in feeds should not exceed four per cent. Usually natural foods provide vitamins in extensive culture systems. But in modified extensive and semi intensive systems of culture, vitamins need to be fortified with diet. Its requirement varies with size, growth rate, environmental conditions etc. Shrimps need 11 water soluble vitamins such as thiamin, riboflavin, pyridoxine, pantothenic acid, niacin, biotin, inositol, choline, folic acid, cynocobalamine, ascorbic acid and 4 fat soluble vitamins such as vitamin-A, vitamin-D, vitamin-E and vitamin-K in the diet (Akiyama *et al.*, 1992).

There are twenty inorganic elements which are required for different functions of body. Some are needed in considerable amounts called as macro-minerals and others in trace quantities called as micro-minerals. The former includes calcium, phosphorus, potassium, magnesium, sodium, chlorine and sulphur while the latter includes iron, copper, zinc, manganese, cobalt, selenium, molybdenum and iodine. Binders are used to provide water stability to feeds. Commonly used binders are wheat flour, alpha-starch, gelatin, collagen, agar, fresh fish flesh etc. Anti oxidants are used to prevent rancidity by lipids and loss of vitamins. Commonly used antioxidants are butylated hydroxyanisole (BHA) and butylated hydroxytoluene (BHT).

In extensive culture, shrimp derive its nutrition from natural feeds available in the pond. In modified extensive and semi intensive systems, shrimp depend on natural pond productivity during early stages but require supplementary feed in final stages. Formulated pellet feeds with four hours of water stability should be used to obtain more production. Feeds should be given in feeding trays in selected places of pond and needs to be monitored regularly. Excess feeding can be avoided by increasing frequency or reducing the amount. It is ideal to provide more feed in evening and night hours than in day time due to nocturnal feeding habit of shrimps.

MONITORING POND ENVIRONMENT

Pond environment influences growth of shrimp by enhancing feed conversion. The environmental factors which affect the growth are temperature, pH, Salinity, dissolved oxygen, pH, carbon dioxide, ammonia, plankton, benthos, organic matter etc. of water as well as texture, soil pH, redox potential, organic carbon of soil.

Temperature of water between 20° to 30° C is suitable. Higher temperature of more than 35° C is lethal. Ideal range of pH is 7 to 9. Salinity of 15 to 30 ppt is suitable. Dissolved oxygen of around 3.5mg/l is good for growth. Carbon dioxide level of below 10 mg/l is not harmful if adequate oxygen is available. The unionized ammonia is toxic and its level of 0.1mg/l adversely affect the growth. Plankton in water causes turbidity and produces oxygen and organic matter. It also absorbs harmful substances and its optimum density can be about 20 to 30 cm in Secchi disc value. Higher visibility indicates inadequate plankton, natural food organisms and threat of macrophyte infestation. Lower value indicates excess plankton and probabilities of oxygen depletion.

Condition of pond bottom is quite important because shrimps are bottom dwellers. It greatly influence growth and survival of shrimps and studies on pond soil is of immense significance in shrimp culture. Shrimp farms are mainly located in coastal areas which has heavy clay soil. Peat soils are not suitable. Brackish water is highly buffered and it is exchanged in shrimp ponds regularly which neutralize acidity. The redox potential is a measure of degree of oxygenation and reduction of the soil. If it is 500 mv (millivolts), then DO (dissolved oxygen) level is high. When it is 340 mv, the DO level is 2 to 3 mg/l and nitrite appears. If it is less than 200mv, then DO level is almost nil and ferrous iron compound give soil black colour. Hydrogen sulfide appears when redox potential drops below 100 mv. A brown surface crust or a crust of the natural soil colour indicates oxidized conditions, while a black surface is a sign of reduced conditions (Boyd and Fast, 1992). It is ideal to dry the bottom soil and plough it after harvest of crop in every year to enhance mineralization of organic load at pond bottom. Lime is applied in pond to correct pH, disinfection and improving mineralization. Its quantity varies as per pH of soil. Organic manures are applied depending on organic carbon content of soil while inorganic fertilizers applied as per nitrogen and phosphorus level.

Guidelines of Aquaculture Authority of India needs to be followed in shrimp farming. It addresses different issues such as environmental impact assessment, CRZ related matters, waste water treatment, licensing, effluent water quality, quarantine, disease certification, use of chemicals and drugs etc.

REFERENCES

Akiyama, D.M.,Dominy, W.G. and Lawrence, A.L. (1992): Penaeid Shrimp Nutrition. In: *Marine Shrimp Culture: Principles and Practices* (A.W.Fast and L.J.Lester, Eds.). Elsivier Publishers,Amsterdam, pp. 535-568.

Boyd, C.E. and Fast, A.W.(1992): Pond Monitoring and Management. In: *Marine Shrimp Culture: Principles and Practices* (A.W. Fast and L.J.Lester, Eds.). Elsivier Publishers, Amsterdam, pp. 497-514.

Fast, A.W. and Lannan, J.E. (1992): Pond Dynamic Processes. In: *Marine Shrimp Culture: Principles and Practices* (A.W.Fast and L.J.Lester, Eds.). Elsivier Publishers, Amsterdam, pp. 431-456.

Ravichandran, P. (2006): Shrimp Farming. In: Hand Book of Fisheries and Aquaculture (Ayyappan, S. Ed.). Indian Council of Agricultural Research, New Delhi, pp. 392-403.

5

Re-visioning the Chilika
A Guide to Opening the Mouth Healing the Lagoon and its Biodiversity in Every Aspect to Rejuvenate its Beauty

Mamini Kumari Maharana[1]
Binod Kumar Maharana[2]
Dr. Lingaraj Patro[3]

ABSTRACT

The hydrological invention taken for the restoration of the Chilika lagoon has resulted in a considerable improvement for its fishery resources, water quality positive impact on the biodiversity and overall improvement of the aquatic ecosystem

1. Lecturer in English, Deccan College, Berhampur, Orissa, India, *E-mail:* mamini.maharana1@gmail.com

2. Environmental Lawyer, Berhampur, Orissa, India, *E-mail:* binod.maharana1@gmail.com

3. Environmental Toxicology Lab, Department of Zoology & Biotechnology, KBDAV College, Nirakapur - 752 019 (Khurda), Orissa, India, *E-mail:* dr.lrpatro@rediffmail.com

of the lagoon. It is always remain one of the hot spot place for the tourist and holiday lovers. The Chilika not only attracts to the nature lovers but also the migrant birds to visit this place every year in the winter season. The Irrawaddy dolphins, crabs and ornamental fish always in hence its beauty. After receiving the prestigious Ramsar Award 2002, Chilika has turned to its pulsing mood. The improvement in the water label variation and the tidal cycle thus making the lagoon more productivity and nursing the water quality with additional nutrients.

Keywords: Chilika, CDA, Ramsar, Wetland, New Mouth, Resources, Aquatic ecosystem, Conservation and Management.

INTRODUCTION

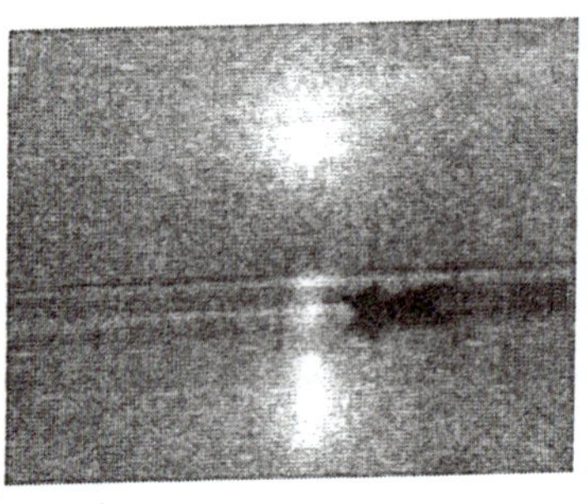

Chilika has a pride of place in Orissa's literature and culture, and has influenced the poets and philosophers. It has great significance for planners, scientists, international organiza-tions such as 'The Wetlands Interna-tional' and 'Asian Wetland Bureau'. Chilika lagoon has been designated as a Ramsar site (Wetland of International importance) from 1st October, 1981. The water spread of the lagoon varies between 1165 sq.km in monsoon to 906 sq.km during summer and extends over Puri, Khurda and Ganjam districts. The lagoon itself can be broadly divided into four natural sectors based on salinity and depth: the southern zone, central zone, northern zone, and the outer channel. Numerous islands are present in the lagoon, prominent among which are Kalijai, Honeymoon, Barakuda, Breakfast, Birds Island, etc. One of the submerged (potential) islands covering, an area of 15.53 sq.km has been notified as Chilika (Nalaban) Wildlife Sanctuary on 17th December 1987. The whole area of the Chilika Lake, excluding the area notified as Sanctuary has been declared as a 'Closed Area' for a period of five years with effect from 16th December 2002. The ecosystem features of Chilika comprising of tidal ingress from the sea, which mixes with the fresh water brought the wetland, in one way or the other for economic activities. About 70% of this population depends on fishing as the means of livelihood.

The Chilika lagoon is hot spot of rich biodiversity. There are 546 species of angiospermic plants belonging by rivers such as Daya, Bhargabi, Luna, and large number of rivulets. Several islands are situated in this lagoon, inhabited by large human population (1.3 lakh approx.) dependent on this wetland for sustenance. A number of villages and towns around the lagoon are closely associated with to 379 genera and 107 families, above 100 phytoplankton genera, 20 species of weed and 7 pteridophytic.

SCOPE OF STUDY

Chilika lagoon, which was fast degrading during the past few decades with rapid adverse changes in its ecological characters, was restored by the Chilika Development Authority during the year 2000-2001. A number of restoration measures were taken be CDA in Chilika lagoon, including the most important hydrological intervention. Due to the most successful eco-restoration measures, CDA bagged the must prestigious Ramsar Wetland Conservation Awarded in 2003 for the first time from among the Asian Countries.

The scope of the present article has covered description of general features of Chilika lagoon, adverse changes in ecological characters and eco-problems before restoration by reviewing the published literatures and undertaking in-depth discussion with the scientific and engineering personnel of CDA, Bhubaneswar. Specific studied through field observation and survey on the following aspects have been covered under the scope of study. They are:

- Field study on the eco-restoration in Chilika
- Impact of restoration measures on eco-system as a whole and its stakeholders.

HISTORY OF CHILIKA

Legend and geology provide interesting contrasts in their versions of the history of Chilika. Legend reveals that the pirate King Raktabahhu came to ransack Puri with a huge fleet of ships. He anchored out of sight to avoid detection, but the sea washed up refuse from the ships to shore and warned the towns people, who fled with all their possessions. Raktabahu thus found a deserted city when he finally arrived. Furious, he insisted that the sea had betrayed him and ordered his army to attack it. The sea entered the seabed in pursuit. Then it surged back, drowning the army and forming what is now Chilika lagoon. Many ancient texts mention the southern sector of Chilika as being a major harbour for many time commerce, back in the days when the King of Kalinga was known as Lord of the Sea. Indeed, some rocks in the Southern sector are marked by a band of white formed by remains of coral (which are exclusively a marine). This band is at a height of 8m above the current water level, a clear indication that the area was once a marine, and the water much deeper that it is today.

Geological studies tell us that the coastline extended along the western shores of Chilika in the Pleistocene era, and that the entire northeastern region above Chilika was under the sea. Since then, the coastline has moved considerably eastward. Similarly, the Konark temple, built on the seashore a few hundred years ago, is now over 3 km from the coast.

Most lagoons seen today were formed as a result of a worldwide rise in sea levels over the past 6,000-8,000 years. There was a pause in the rise in sea levels about 7,000 years ago, when a sandy beach might have formed near the coast at the Southern sector, As the sea rose further, this sand beach grew gradually. It progressed seaward and to the northeast, to form what is now the spit of Chilika. A recent fossil from the southwestern edge of the spit has been dated to about 3,500-4,000 years ago, which is some indication of how long ago the lagoon was formed (Venkataratnam 1970). The growth of the spit at Chilika is supposed to be due to the abrupt change in the direction of the coast north of the lake, strong winds transferring sand to the shore, long shore drift, and the presence or absence of strong river and tidal currents in different areas.

The spit of Chilika is constantly changing. The sand bar has been wide-ning, and the posi-tion of the mouth constantly shifting, moving generally towards the north-east. The mouth was descri-bed as being about 1.5 km wide in 1780, and had decreased to half that within forty years (Hunter 1872). The mouth frequently gets choked up and has to be cut open artificially, often by the local fisher folk, whose livelihood depends critically on maintaining an access for the sea to enter Chilika. Meanwhile the former seabed that is now Chilika is being gradually silted up by the rivers running into it, converting, the lagoon into its present shallow state.

Chilika is an integral part of the culture of coastal Orissa. Almost 400 years ago, the saint poet Purshottam Das, a devotee of Lord Jagannath, wrote a poem about Lord Krishna dancing with a milkmaid called Maniki, who had come to sell curds on the banks of the Chilika. Even today, a village Manikagauda (gauda being the cowherd caste) stands on Chilika lagoon. More recently, the great Oriya poet, Radhanath Rai, fascinated by the beauty of the lagoon, wrote an epic poem 'Chilika" which is regarded as a masterpiece of descriptive geography. The freedom fighter Gopabandhu Das (know as "Orissa's Gandhi"), in his book *"Bandir Atmakatha"* ("Autobiography of a prisoner"), wrote eloquently about Chilika viewed from a train travelling along its banks in the 1920s.

When the British invaded Orissa from the south in 1803, the traitor Fateh Muhammed met them on the shores of Chilika. He showed them the eastern route, by which they managed to reach Puri undetected. In, return, Fateh Muhammed was given freehold of the areas of Malud and Parikud, most of which is today called Garh Krishnaprasad block.

The British and settlement for Orissa in 1897-98 recorded the exclusive enjoyment of fisheries in Chilika by the fishermen community. The fisheries of Chilika were part of the Zamindari estates of Khallikote, Parikud, Suna Bibi, Mirza Taher Baig and the Chaudhary families of Bhungarpur and the Khas mahal areas of Khurda, lying within the kingdoms of the Rajas of Parikud and Khallikote. The zamindars used to lease out the fisheries exclusively to the local fisherfolk. The Birtish also started a Cooperative store in Balugaon in 1926 to provide fishing equipment to locals. In addition, the British constituted 25 Primary Fishermen Cooperatives during the World War II.

During these centuries of exclusive rights, fisher folk evolved a complex system of partitioning the fisheries of Chilika amongst themselves. Several castes of fisherfolk developed a large array of fishing techniques, nets and gear. According to the fisherfolk the harvested the lake in a relatively sustainable fashion. After the abolition of zamindari in 1953, traditional fishing areas continued to be leased out to cooperatives of local fishermen. As fishing (particularly prawn fishing) becomes increasingly remunerative, outside interests began entering the area.

The leasing system broke down completely in 1991 when the Orissa government outlined leasing policy that would in essence have resulted in the auction of leases to the highest bidder. The cooperatives challenged the order in court, and the

Orissa High Court directed the Government to make changes that would safeguard traditional fishermen's interests. However, no new lease have been issued to date. As a result, chaos reigns and the local people are being marginalized by powerful outsiders.

Recently the Government of Orissa has issued a notification banning the lease of Chilika for culture fishery.

WELCOME TO CHILIKA

Chilika is the largest lagoon along the east coast of India, situated between latitude 19° 28′ and 19° 54′ N and longitude 85° 05′ and 85° 38′ E. The lagoon is a unique assemblage of marine, brackish and fresh water eco-system with estuarine characters. It is one of the hotspots of biodiversity and shelters a number of endangered species listed in the IUCN red list of threatened species, and also is a designated Ramsar site. It is an avian grandeur and the wintering ground for more than one million migratory birds. The highly productive lagoon eco-system with its rich fishery resources sustains the livelihood of more than 0.15 million-fisher folk who live in and around the Lagoon. The water spread area of the Lagoon varies between 1165 to 906 sq.km during the monsoon and summer respectively. A 32-km long, narrow, outer channel connects the lagoon to the Bay of Bengal, near the village Motto, recently a new mouth was opened by CDA which has brought a new lease of life to the lagoon.

The total number of fish species are reported to be 225 . Along with a variety of phytoplankton, algae and aquatic plants, the Lagoon region also supports over 720 species of non-aquatic plants (CDA). A survey of the fauna of Chilika carried out by the Zoological Survey of India in 1985-87 recorded over 800 species in and around the lagoon. This list

includes a number of rare, threatened and endangered species, including the Barakudia limbless skink. On account of its rich bio-diversity, Chilika was designated as a "Ramsar Site", i.e. a wetland of international Importance. The Nalaban Island within the Lagoon is notified as a Bird Sanctuary under Wildlife (Protection) Act, the lagoon is also identified as a priority site for conservation and management by the National Wetland Coral Reefs Committee of Ministry of Environment and Forests, Government of India. The Lagoon is a highly productive ecosystem and with it's rich fishery resources sustains the livelihood of more than 1,50,000 fisher folk who live in and around the lagoon. The mouth connecting the channel to the sea is close to the northeastern end of the Lagoon.

ECOLOGICAL CHARACTERISTICS AND ISSUES

As a background to defining current resource management problems within Chilika Lagoon, this section of the report describes the Lagoon ecosystem and the current status of the aquatic resources. Relevant features of the ecosystem directly supporting, or contributing to fisheries and aquaculture production, are highlighted.

This includes a consideration of general features of lagoon ecology, followed by a systematic review of information pertaining to lower trophic levels and commercial aquatic resources. This is followed by; an evaluation of several different forms of aquaculture of present or potential significance within Chilika Lake.

GENERAL LAGOON ECOLOGY

High nutrient concentrations are often present in Lagoons as a result of both riverine nutrient inputs and effective nutrient recycling between the sediments and the water column. Lagoons are, therefore, often highly productive aquatic environments. A comparison of productivity land biomass estimates for lagoons around the world (Tables 5.1 and 5.2) clearly indicates that Lagoons are characterized by exceptionally high productivity and biomass, compared to other aquatic ecosystems. The following features provide lagoons with their distinctive characteristics.

Table 5.1: The fish prawn and crab landings of 2001-02 and 2002-03

All time lowest landing of fish and prawn in 1995-96	1269 MT
All time high fish and prawn landing in 2001-2002	11,877.81 MT
All time high prawn landing in 2002-2003	2478.82 MT
All time high crab landing in 2002-2003	149.81 MT
Three years average fish landings after opening of the new mouth (Table 5.1)	9,170.30 MT. (+ 428.02% growth over the base year 1999-2000)
Average prawn landing during last 3 years (post-intervention period)	2040.94 MT. (Highest growth of + 1031.4% over the base year 1999-2000)
Low priced freshwater elements in the fish landingsare gradually decreasing during last 3 years, which is improving the catch quality.	
Economic valuation of fish, prawn and crab landings during 2001-2002 - Rs. 57.16 Crores during 2002-2003 - Rs. 55.38 Crores	- Rs. 57.16 Crores - Rs. 55.38 Crores
Value realised from export of 1239.41MT of prawn and 36.23 MT crab to foreign markets during 2001-02	Rs. 23.51 Crores
Fishery productivity during 2001-2002 - 129.96 kg. ha-1" 2002-2003	118.09 kg. ha-1

(Contd...)

Catch Per Unit Effort (CPUE) -2001-2002 2002-2003	- 6.89 kg. boat-1 day-1 - 6.32 kg. boat-1 day-1
Estimated economic loss due to destructive fishing (Juvenile Killing) - 151.04 Mt. juveniles value	Rs. 8.35 Crores
Estimated per-capita income of fishers during 2001-02	Rs. 19,575
Export of fresh fish to other states (West Bengal,AP, Jharkhand, TamilNadu, Kerala, MP, Chhattisgarh, Maharastra & New Delhi) during 2001-2002	6423.59 MT.

Table 5.2: The sector-wise results of the census -2007

Sector	*Annual census of Irrawaddy dolphins recorded in Chilika Lagoon (Conducted on 20th Feb.2007)*			
	Adults	*Sub adults*	*Calves*	*Total*
Southern sector	26	5	1	32
Central sector	18	6	0	24
Northern sector	06	0	0	06
Outer channel	65	4	4	73
Total	115	15	5	135

- The high degree of shelter from tidal and current action;
- The relatively stable salinity gradients;
- The soft mud and/or sand substrates;
- The well-mixed nature of the water column through wind action;
- Extreme shallowness;
- Organic richness;
- Rapidity with which they change (over geological time scales).

In climates with seasonal rainfall, and where major inputs of freshwater exist a pronounced seasonal variation in salinity and/or water level. In comparison with estuaries, contributions of phyto-plankton and submerged macro-phytes in lagoons are more impor-tant in production processes. Most of the production is consumed within the system, and there is less export of nutrients and organic material due to the closed nature of lagoons and of the unimportance of tidal fluxes. Carbon sources include phytoplankton, benthic and epiphytic algae and detritus derived

from macrophytes. The latter detrital source is especially important as a source of carbon. The pond weed, *Potamogeton pectinatus* decays very rapidly within the lagoon environment. Studies suggest that under environmental conditions of 15-26° C temperature and 5-11 ppt salinity, most nutrient release from *Potamogeton* occurred during its first week of decay, and decay processes very largely complete within 128 days. Within lagoons, detrital enrichment via bacterial heterotrophs is the dominant trophic pathway supplying energy to biological consumers.

Most of the consumers are thought to acquire detritus, benthic algae and epiphytes in an indiscriminate fashion via deposit feed and/or browsing. Among vertebrates within lagoons (both birds and fish) most species are opportunistic omnivores or carnivores.

In summary, lagoons are extremely productive environments due largely to high nutrient inputs from surrounding land drainages, as well as efficient nutrient re-cycling. This high productivity supports lagoon fisheries for both fish and shell fish. Lagoons are ephemeral environments (on geological time scales) evolving rapidly into other types of semi-aquatic, habitats (marshes, swamps). Simultaneous with this succession is a gradual shift from high salinity conditions to freshwater. Human activities within lagoon watersheds often serve to increase the succession rate of lagoons towards their ultimate terrestrial end-state. Virtually all of these general processes appear to be currently operating within Chilika Lake.

SILTATION

Soil erosion is prevalent in the catchments of Chilika due to over-grazing, illicit felling, cultivation along hill slopes, and clearance of vegetation for rehabilitation and agriculture. About 365,000 tonnes of sediment is now added annually to the lake through streams of various sizes. This has resulted in siltation, reducing the area of the inlet and natural connection to the sea.

Restriction of the hydraulic capacity of the inlet that connects the lake to the sea has reduced flushing of the lake and has led to a decrease in salinity and the loss of some marine and brackish water species from the ecosystem.

WEED INFESTATION

Increased siltation and decreased salinity has promoted the spread of major weed species more tolerant of fresh and brackish water. These include *Eichhornia crassipes, Azolla pinnata,* and *Potamogeton pectinatus*. Weed infestation increased from 20 km^2 in 1973 to nearly 400 km^2 in 1993. The increased coverage has occurred mainly in the northwestern end of the lagoon and has restricted the feeding and breeding grounds of many fish of economic importance, and has also restricted the free flow of sediment.

BIRD HUNTING

For some years, many villagers from the adjoining villages had been poaching birds from the lake as their sole means of livelihood. This activity was a serious threat to the populations of some species and severely disturbed many other species which roosted or fed in the lake.

POLLUTION

Although water pollution from industrial sources is not a major problem around the lake, fertilizer and pesticide residues from nearby agricultural fields pose a serious problem in the northern part of the lake. Similarly, sewage and the waste water from the peripheral small villages and towns, including Balugaon and Rambha, is posing a pollution problem, although at present it is not considered a significant threat. In summary, although pollution is not yet seen as a major problem for Chilika, it has the potential to increase, and management responses may become increasingly necessary.

OLD MOUTH

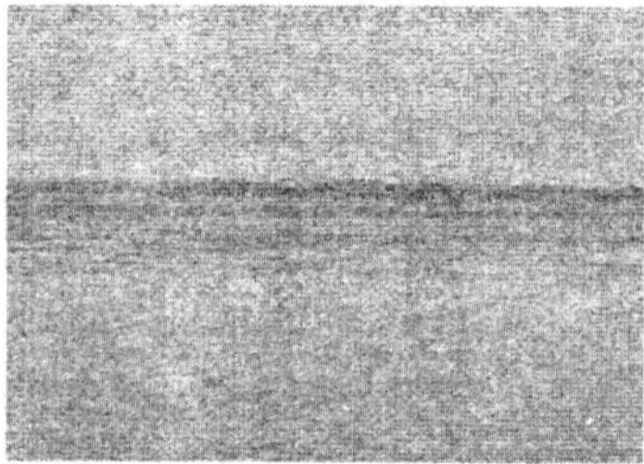

View showing the problem of siltation in the shallow areas, due to which the old mouth of the bay was choked, causing ecological problems

RESTORATION

Chilika is the largest lagoon along the east coast of India and a Ramsar site. Chilika is a unique assemblage of marine, brackish and fresh water eco-system with estuarine characters and is a hotspot of biodiversity that shelters a number of endangered species listed in the IUCN red list of threatened species. It is an avian grandeur and the wintering ground for more than one million migratory bird. The highly productive eco-system of the lagoon with its rich fishery resources sustains the livelihood of more than 0.15 million fisher folk who live in and around the lagoon. Chilika ecosystem had been encountering a number of problem and threat like – siltation, shrinkage of water spread area, choking of the inlet channel as well as shifting of the mouth connecting to the sea, decrease in salinity and fishery resources, proliferation of fresh water invasive species, and an over-all loss of biodiversity more so the decline in the productivity adversely affecting the livelihood of the community who depend on it. The lagoon was placed in the Montreux record in the year 1993 by Ramsar bureau due to change in its ecological characters. Being concerned with the degradation of the lagoon ecosystem Chilika Development Authority (CDA) was created in1992, for restoration and overall development of the lagoon.

The spatial and temporal salinity gradients that exist in Chilika give it the unique characteristics of an estuarine eco-system, exercising a continuous and selective influence on its biota. The transformation of the lagoon towards a fresh water ecosystem was considered as a potential threat to its unique ecosystem. To address this problem, CDA commissioned the services of the premier institutes of the country like National Institute of Oceanography, (NIO) Goa, to study the wave climate of the inlet, long shore sediment transport along the shore and the bathymetry of the lead channel. The Central Water and Power Research Station (CWPRS), Pune, carried out the hydrological and two dimensional mathematical model studies. The studies concluded that the tidal influx into the lagoon was considerably reduced because of the shoal formation along the lead channel and continuous shifting of the mouth that resulted in significant hydraulic head loss.

NEW MOUTH

Opening of a New Mouth Opposite to Village Sipakuda

As per the findings of the CWPRS, Pune, it was concluded that the salinity flux and tidal flux into the lagoon would not improve unless the location of the lagoon mouth get closer to the lagoon proper. Based on their three dimensional numerical model studies, they recommended that an experimental mouth with 100M width and 2.5M below the lowest lagoon water level must be dredged, so that the salinity flux into the lagoon would improve by 40% and the tidal flux would improve by 45%. This would rejuvenate the Lagoon ecosystem and the desired level of salinity i.e., 15 ppt during summer in northern sector can be achieved. Accordingly the opening to the sea was also accomplished opposite to the village Sipakuda on 23rd September 2000. This was carried out as per the technical guidance of the CWPRS, Pune as well as Ocean Engineering Centre, IITM, Chennai. NIO Goa carried out the monitoring of the lagoon. After the desiltation, the monitoring of the lagoon is carried out to assess the impact of the desiltation by National Institute of Oceanography, Goa to assess the impact of the opening of the mouth on the lagoon eco system. The close monitoring of the lagoon is also carried out by CDA at an interval of thirty days.

IRS 1D LISS III IMAGE OF CHILIKA LAGOON

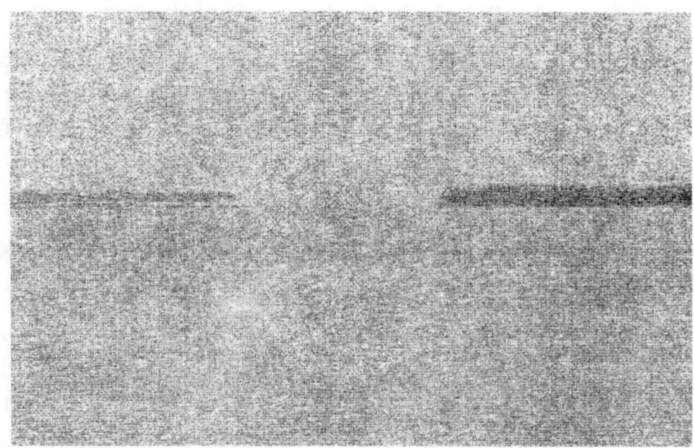

PHASE-II OF DESILTATION

The major rivers such as Daya, Bhargavi and Luna the distributaries of Mahanadi river system drain in to the lagoon in the northern sector. These river systems drain 4385 million cumec of fresh water into the lagoon. The bed sediments like clay, silt and pebbles, (the higher gravity particles) brought by the above rivers are deposited in the river mouth. Based on the model studies the Central Water and Power Research Station, Pune have further recommended that the area adjoining to Daya, Bhargabi outfall point is remaining fresh-water up to Barakudi, and is also totally infested with fresh water weed, which is also obstructing the free flow of water and sediment. Therefore, they have recommended extension of the dredge channel from Muggermukh to the river confluence point of the Daya and Bhargavi over a length of 22.6 km. The extension work is now in progress and expected to be completed by August, 2003. It is predicted that the channel will have the following positive impacts:

- The channel will facilitate free flow of fresh water from the rivers draining to the Chilika and will be helpful in maintaining the mouth. Due to efficient disposal of flood water, the water logging problem along the north-western periphery of the lagoon will reduce.

- The channel will help in flushing-out of the sediment.
- Due to the propagation of the salinity the fresh-water invasive species growing in the northern sector will reduce, and the water spread area of more than hundred square kilometres will become free from fresh waterweed. It will also facilitate the migration of Hilsa fish.

IMPACT OF THE DESILTATION AND NEW MOUTH ON CHILIKA ECOSYSTEM

The opening of the artificial mouth is considered as an historic and successful intervention in the history of the restoration of the eco system of the wetlands in India, which is evident from the following positive impacts, which are noticed after the desiltation of the outer channel as well as the opening of the new mouth.

Salinity

The northern sector of the lagoon was remaining freshwater almost through out the year, but after the opening of the mouth, the salinity level of the northern sector improved appreciably to, 26.2, 21.2 and 31.2 ppt, at station no. 17, 18 and 19 respectively, during the month of May 2001, against the average salinity level of 0.5 to 2.5 ppt recorded during the same period in past one decade (Fig. 5.1).

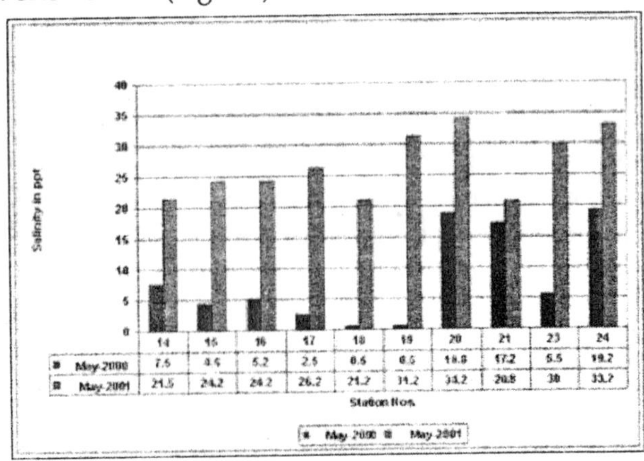

Fig. 5.1: Variation of salinity in the northern sector (2000-01)

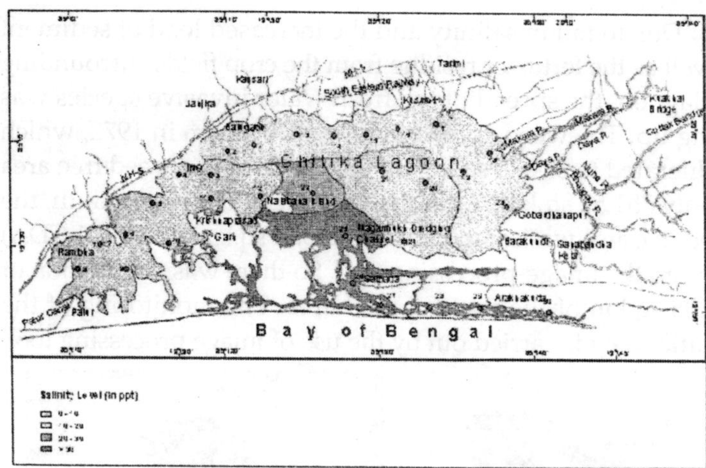

Fig. 5.2: Salinity Level (Pre-Monsoon-May-2000) before opening of New mouth

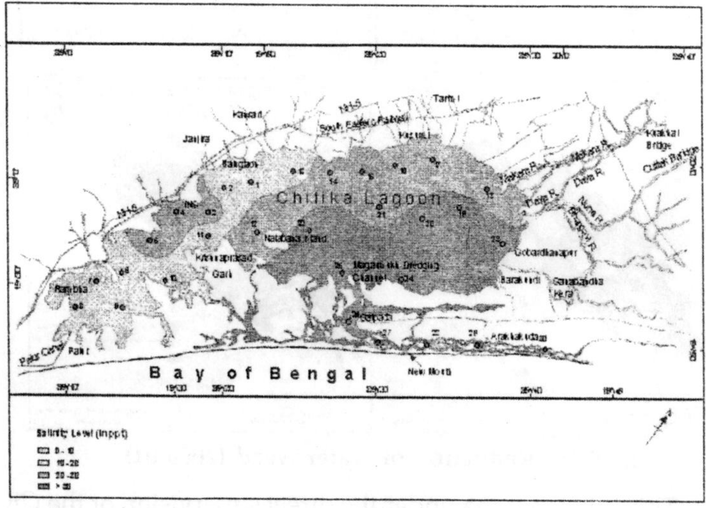

Fig. 5.3: Salinity Level - (Pre-Monsoon-May-2001)

REDUCTION OF FRESH WATER WEED

Due to fall in salinity and the increased load of sediment as well as the fertilizer residue from the crop fields surrounding the lagoon, the spread of the fresh water invasive species was going up. The weed spread area was 20 sq.km in 1972, which proliferated to 684.70 sq.km in May 2000, with a weed free area of only 351.51 sq.km. After the opening of the new mouth, the weed free area was computed to be 508.51 sq.km (May 2001 CDA) through the image-processing unit. So there was a reduction of 157.05 sq.km of the weed spread area. The monitoring of the aquatic weed is carried out by the use of image processing tool.

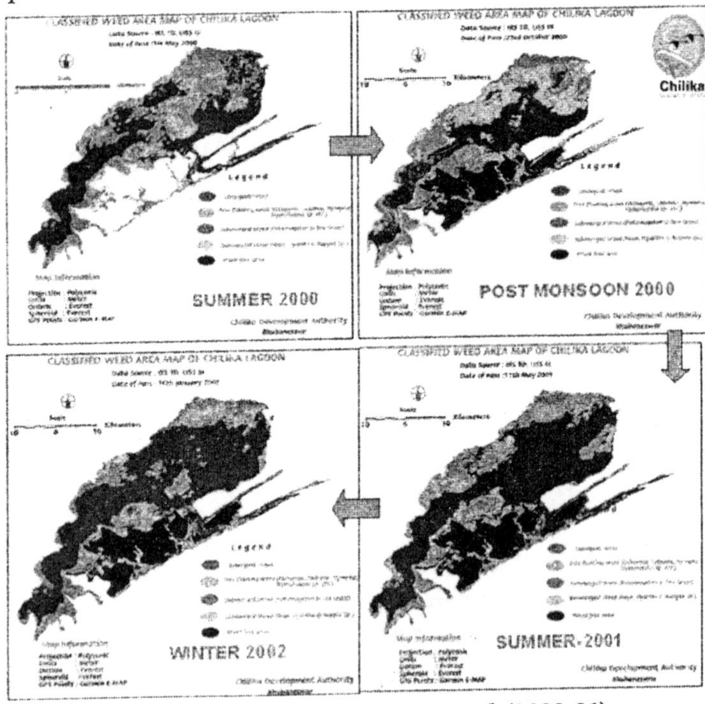

Fig. 5.4: Reduction of water weed (2000-01)

This is being done under the direct supervision of the CE, CDA. One of the most positive finding is that the invasive species like water hyacinth is reducing which are replaced by the reed (Phragmites karka).

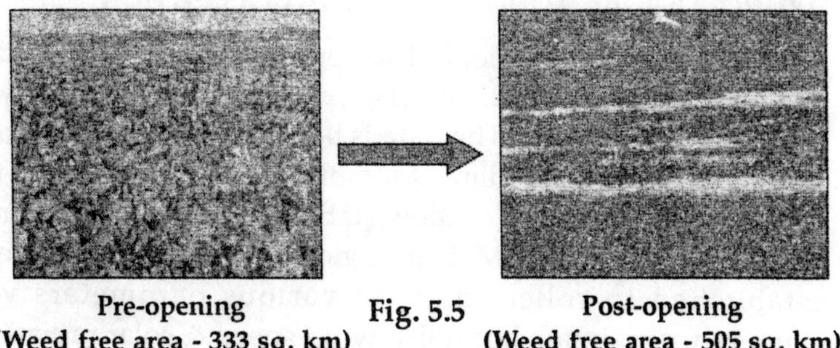

Pre-opening (Weed free area - 333 sq. km) Fig. 5.5 Post-opening (Weed free area - 505 sq. km)

FORMATION OF SEAGRASS MEADOWS

Sea grasses are the sole marine representatives of the angiosperms. One of the most productive ecosystems on earth is the sea grass meadow. These are encountered in estuaries, lagoons, and shallow open shelves off the seacoast, which serve as nursery ground for a large number of fish and invertebrate species, and provide the critical habitat for dugongs and turtles. They also play an important role in the food web of inshore coastal areas. Prior to the opening of the new mouth of the lagoon, the most common sea grass species recorded was *Halophila ovalis* (paddle weed), which is more tolerant of low salinities and low light condition, than other sea grass species. The distribution of the above species was also poor and extremely patchy in the lagoon. Small beds of *Ruppia maritima* were observed to be common in the shallow waters of southern and central sectors in association with *Halophila* sp. mostly along the shoreline. After opening of the mouth the species, diversity of the sea grass is being observed to be improving as three new species of sea grasses. *Halophila* is also recorded for the first time in the deep waters from the creeks of the Krushna Prasad Island with prolific growth during post monsoon months forming extensive meadows. The opening of the new mouth provided stable salinity regime with less fluctuations, improved water clarity, especially during post monsoon and summer months, which are perhaps the reason for the luxuriant growth and formation of sea grass meadows.

HYDROLOGICAL MONITORING DATA COLLECTION

Hydrometry: Hydrological stations have been established in and around Chilika Lake to collect data on inflow/outflow of fresh and saline water. The data is being collected thrice a day for all the stream and sediment sampling (inflow) stations. In the stream gauging inflow/outflow stations, data is collected once a day during low tide. Meteorological stations have also been established to collect data on various parameters viz. temperature, rainfall, humidity, wind speed & solar radiation. Details of the stations are as under:

- Eleven stream gauging and sediment sampling stations (inflow) have been established at Balkati, Goardhanpur, Andarasungh, Samantrapur, Jankir, Chupuring, Tarimi, Baddiha, Kumbhirapada, Chherapadara and Langaleswar four inflow/flow monitoring stations have been installed in the outer channel at Magarmukh, Sipakuda, Palur and Arkhakuda.
- Two meteorological yards have been set up at INS premises and Satapada .
- Rain gauge stations have been installed at 3 locations at Balugaon.

KALIJAI AND KRISHNAPRASAD GARH

Data on water discharge and sediment load is also being procured from a network of stations established by Water Resource Department, Government of Orissa to determine the impacts of water resources developmental activities within the river basin on Chilika Lagoon.

WATER QUALITY

Data on water quality is being collected from 30 stations in the lagoon to monitor changes in the physico-chemical parameters of water. The monitoring is being carried out on monthly basis. The parameters being estimated among others are atmospheric temperature, water temperature, turbidity, total suspended solids (TSS), pH, conductivity, alkalinity, salinity, dissolved oxygen (DO), BOD, nitrate, orthophosphate, sodium and potassium.

A well-equipped laboratory has been set up in Bhubaneswar with facilities of water quality analysis, hydrological analysis, biological characteristics, fisheries assessment etc. In addition to this, an on-site laboratory has also been set up in Balugaon.

International Acclaim for Unique Eco-Restoration of Chilika Lagoon (Ramsar Wetland Conservation Award)

The Ramsar Wetland Conservation Award was established in 1969 by the Convention on Wetlands to recognize and honour individuals, organizations, and government agencies every three years that have made a significant contribution to wetland conservation and sustainable use in any part of the world. The Ramsar Wetlands Awards for 2002 is conferred to the Chilika Development Authority in view of its outstanding achievements in the field of restoration way in which local communities have been included in these activities. The award also includes the Evian Special Prize consisting of US$ 10,000 generously donated by the Danone Group as part of a collaborative project with the Ramsar Convention. The CDA is the first organization from Asia to receive this prestigious award. The Ramsar Award was presented to the CDA at the opening ceremony of the eighth Meeting of the Conference of the Parties to the Convention, (COP-8) at Valencia, Spain on 18 November 2002.

FISH YIELD STATUS IN CHILIKA LAGOON DURING POST-HYDROLOGICAL INTERVENTION PERIOD (2001-02-2002-03)

Chilika lagoon with high biological productivity is a nature's bountiful and varied gift of aquatic living resources to mankind. Being influenced by tidal influx from the sea and freshwater inflow from rivers and catchments, the sector, central, southern and outer channel sectors, which are characterized with different and ratio-temporal salinity pattern

fauna. The lagoon has been providing food and livelihood security to more than 1.5 lakh fishers living in its 132 peripheral and island villages.

Species Richness (Fishery biodiversity)

Fisheries wealth of Chilika lagoon comprises of 323 species (updated record till 2002) which includes 261 fish species, 28 prawns and 34 crab species, from among the large spectrum of fish species prawn and species only 11 groups from fish, five species from prawn and only two from crab species are commercially important.

Threatened Species and Their Re-appearance

The incessant anthropogenic pressure and several natural upheavals during the past few decades have altered its natural attributes and in the process the fisheries resources have been the worst causality resulting in declining fish landings and significant transformation of fishery with the replacement of saline migratory species by the uneconomic freshwater species. Under the impact of eco-degradation six number of eco-sensitive species because threatened which were rarely seen in the catches during the last couple of decades, they are namely:

1. Chanoschanos (Sebakhainga)
2. Megalopscyprinoids (Panialehio)
3. Elopsmachnata (Nahama)
4. Rhabdosargusberda (Kalakhuranti)
5. Hilsa (Tenuealosa) ilisha (ilishi)
6. Rhinomugilcosula (Kekenda)

The above threatened species have re-appeared in the lagoon after hydrological intervention (eco-restoration meadows) during 2000-01 to 2002-03. Occurrence of their juveniles and adults in the lagoon in the lagoon (captured during seed abundance survey) indicates that their seed incursion into the lake has taken place and their fishery is gradually being established.

Status and Trend of Fish, Prawn and Crab Landings during the Period of Post-Hydrological Intervention

Before the hydrological intervention during September 2000, fish landings in the Chilika lagoon fluctuated between 8872 MT (1986-87) and 1269 MT (1995-96). Similarly, crab landings fluctuated between 141.4 MT (1983-84) and 3.0 MT (1994 -95). After opening of the new mouth and dredging of silt-choked Magarmukh in September, 2000 the fish, prawn and crab landings registered spectacular leap ranging from 93.54 MT to 149.81 MT (crab) during 2000-01 to 2002-03 (Tables 5.1 and 5.2).

Highlights of Present Fish, Prawn and Crab Landings

Fish landing during 2000-01 has been the all time high record being 11,877.81 MT which was most likely due to effective recruitment of fishes from the sea through the new mouth and elevated salinity regime. Although fish landing during 2002-03 was dropped marginally with negative growth of 9.55% as compared to the fish landing in 2001-02, the prawn landing (2478.82 MT) during 2002-03 has registered all time high record (Table 5.2). Crab landing during 2002-03 has also registered all time high record being 149.81 MT.

New Fisheries Research/Investigation Programmes

Three new fisheries investigation programmes have been taken up in Chilika lagoon which has significance in the context of changing ecosystem.

The programme are:

Studies on spawning grounds and seed abundance of fish and prawns in the Chilika lagoon.

Such studies were made 44 years back by the central inland Fisheries Research Institute, Barrackpore (WB). Since the lagoon has undergone massive ecological change during the period habitat attractions, changes in recruitment pattern and seed abundance etc are most likely. Hence a fresh shady is needed. The programme has been initiated since July 2002. Investigations in four sectors are carried out under regular monthly programmes.

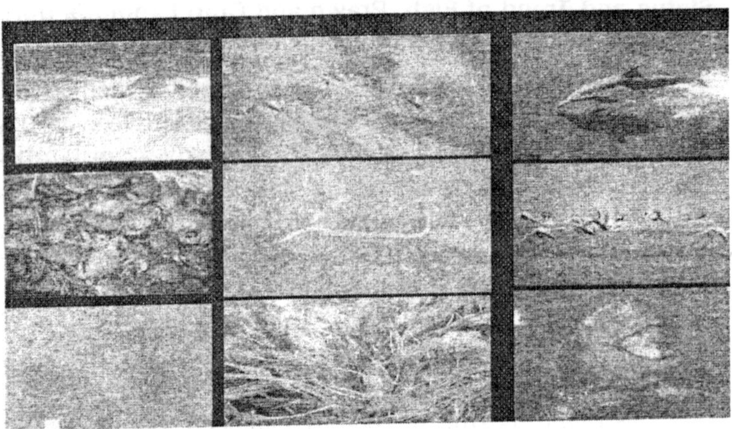

Till now, spawning grounds of most of the economic fishes have been located and studied. Seasonal abundance and distribution of seeds, spawning season of different species are being studied. Studies on ecology, potential fishery and biology of Mud crab sp. (*Scylla* sp.) of Chilika lagoon and their experimental cage culture.

This ecology and fishery of Chilika crab (*Scylla* sp.) including their biological aspects were not studied in the past and therefore information on crab fishery, except landing statistics, were not available. This project has therefore assumed importance.

Till now, a 4-month cage culture experiment of two Scylla species (Red mud Green crab of Chilika) has been completed with encouraging results. Computed yield in six experimental cages ranged from 2526.66 kg/ha/4 months to 5826.67 Kg/ha/4 month and survival ranged from 48.89% to 80.0%. Analysing carapace width and body weight date has established the CW_BW equations for Chilika species, Food and feeding habits, sex ratios, fecundity, maturity index, fishery season, fishing methods, seed incursion and abundance studies are in progress.

- Migration study of three commercially importance fishes (*Mugil uphaus, E. tetra dactylus* and *Hilsa (Temuralosa) ilisha)* through tagging experiment.

This programme is to be taken up during the coming winter season; after the 'Floy-Tanchor' tags (imported) are procured from a USA company arrangement is being made to import the tags.

Crab Landing

The crab landing was recorded to be 79 metric tons during 1985-86 but it decreased sharply to three metric tons during the year 1994-95. After the opening of the mouth i.e. during the year 2000-01 due to the abundant recruitment of the crab juvenile into the lagoon the crab landing touched 93.54 MTs, 111.07 MT in 2001-2002 and 149.81 MT during the year 2002-2003, which is the all time high for past one decade.

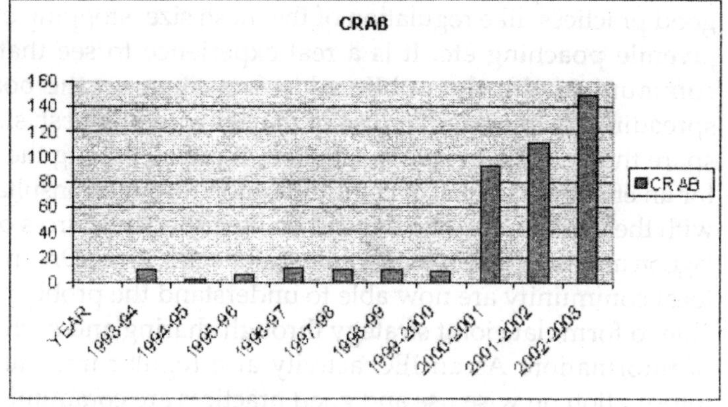

Fig. 5.6: Annual Crab landing from Chilika Lake

Re-appearance of Threatened Species

After opening of the mouth, six species of fish (Hilsa *(Tenualosa)* ilisha, *Megalops cyprinoides, Elops machnata, Chanos chanos, Rhinomugil corsula, Rhabdosargus berda)*, and two species of prawn (*Penaeus indicus and Metpenaeus monoceros)* which had disappeared from the lagoon, reappeared. The total landing of this species during June and July 2000 was recorded to be 438 MT including 200 MT of *Penaeus indicus* which is higher than the last 6 years total annual landing of prawn from capture source.

Migration of Fish

After opening of the new mouth, the distance between the lagoon and the opening to the sea is decreased by 18 km (the distance between old mouth and new mouth) this is facilitating the migration of the *catadramous* and *anadramous* species in to the lagoon. The average salinity level of northern sector during summer improved to 15 ppt against the recorded salinity level of 2-5 ppt during past few decades.

Good Practices

The increase in the fishery resources facilitated the conducive atmosphere for the community to adopt self initiated good practices, like regulation of the mesh size, stopping of the juvenile poaching etc. It is a real experience to see that the community with the public address system on the boat is spreading the message for use of the net with big mesh size to spare the juvenile in side the lagoon. It is also paving the way for an effective channel of communication through consultation with the community who depend on the fishery resources of the lagoon and to adopt co-management strategies. The CDA and the local community are now able to understand the problem and able to formulate joint strategy through sharing and exchange of information. As an IEC activity at a regular interval, the information on wise use and good practices are communicated through the newsletter and pamphlets in local language by CDA.

Annual Population Census of Irrawaddy Dolphins in Chilika Lagoon-2007

The Chilika lagoon is the natural abode of Irrawaddy dolphins and also the cetacean is the flagship species of Chilika. It is a highly endangered species and the total population in the world is estimated to be less than 1000. In India, the Irrawaddy dolphins are only found in Chilika lagoon and it is the largest lagoon population in the world.

The census of Irrawaddy dolphins in Chilika Lagoon was conducted on 20th February, 2007 (Table 5.2).

The sectors of the lagoon were sub divided into 18 zones. The method of line transect survey was adopted. The census works in each zone was carried out by a team of 4-5 experienced persons. Each team was equipped with a boat, binoculars, GPS set, thermometer, water sample bottle and data recording sheets etc. In total, 83 persons from different organizations such as Chilika Wildlife Division, Khurda Forest Division, Chief Wildlife Warden Office, Chilika Development Authority, Centre for Environment Education, NGOs, Researchers, Regional Museum of Natural History, OSDMA, Veterinary department officials, Watershed Mission Officials, lectures from different colleges etc. participated in the census operation. The survey was carried out from 6.30 AM to 3PM on 20th February, 2007. 135 Dolphins were sighted in 4 sectors of Chilika Lagoon. There has been a marginal increase in the number of dolphins recorded past year (131 in 2006).

The marginal increase in the dolphin population has been possible due to close cooperation of the local fishermen community and tourist boat operators. For conservation of dolphins and creating awareness, the CDA has initiated training and sensitization programmes for fishermen and boatmen. The boat operators have been sensitized and advised to attach propeller guards in their boats to prevent injuries to dolphins. In close cooperation with the Wildlife Wing, an enforcement team has been constituted for the protection of the dolphins under Wildlife (Protection) Act, 1972.

Expansion of Irrawaddy Dolphin Distribution

Irrawady dolphin *(Orcaella brevirostris)* is considered as a flagship species of Chilika. Only two lagoon populations of Irrawady dolphins are known in the world; in Chilika lagoon, Orissa, India and Songkhla lagoon, Thailand. Records of distribution are relatively few, although there are some areas of local abundance. Before opening of the mouth most of the dolphins used to be sighted only along the inlet channel and in a limited portion of the central sector of the lagoon. After the opening of the mouth the Irrawady dolphins were observed to be well distributed in the central and the southern sector of the lagoon. This can be attributed due to the improvement in the water quality, food abundance and decrease of the area covered by weed after opening of the new mouth.

Fig. 5.7: Dolphin

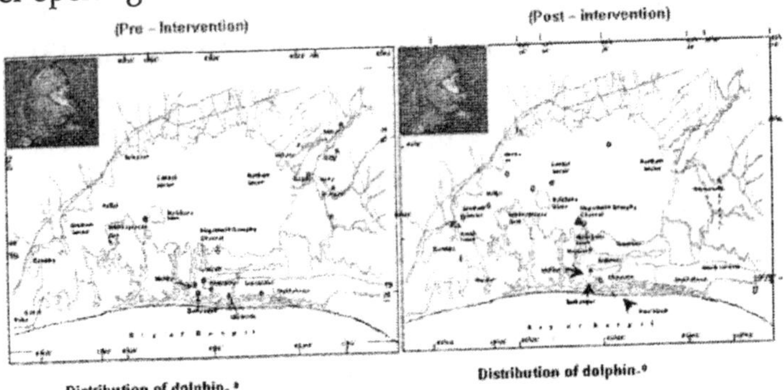

Fig. 5.8: Distribution of Dolphins

BIRDS CENSUS IN CHILIKA LAGOON, 2008

The bird census - 2008 in Chilika lagoon was conducted jointly by the Chilika Development Authority and Orissa State Wildlife Organization on 5th January 2008. The total of 85 personnel and bird experts from Government and non-government organizations (NGOs) such as Bombay Natural History Society, Regional Museum of Natural History, World Wide Fund for

Nature, State Pollution Control Board, Wild Orissa, Wildlife Society of Orissa and experts from Universities and colleges participated in the said Annual Census of Birds. For census propose, the lagoon was divided strategically into seventeen units which included four units in Nalabana birds sanctuary. Each unit was lead by an Ornithologist supported by two to three co-experts. Each census units was provided with a census kit, map of the area, one GPS set, VHF set, Binocular/telescope, reference bird book, water fowl census forms etc. The total bird count was carried out for all bird water bird species and wetland dependant birds through out the lake. Total counts were made for small flocks and larger birds while estimate were made for larger flocks. The time chosen for bird count was from 0700 hours to 1230 hours.

The entire operations was coordinated and monitored by the Chief Executive, CDA, the DFO, Chilika Wildlife Division, Balugaon. The technical inputs were provided by Dr. S. Balachandran, Senior Scientist, BNHS, Dr. U.N. Dev, Ornithologist, Dr. S.K. Kar, Senior Research Officer from Wildlife Originations and Dr. S. Panda, Chief Executive, CDA.

A total of 8.928 lakhs birds belonging to 168 species were counted from the Chilika lagoon as compared to 8.39 lakhs birds enumerated in Jan 2007. The bird's population in Nalabana Bird sanctuary has been recorded as 4.04 lakhs as compared to 1.98lakhs during January 2007.

The species-wise counts indicate that Gadwall ducks were the predominant among all the species numbering more than 1.69 lakhs. The population of other species which exceeded one lakh in numbers was Northern Pintails and Northern Shovellers. The number of birds counted that exceeded 50,000 were *Euresian*

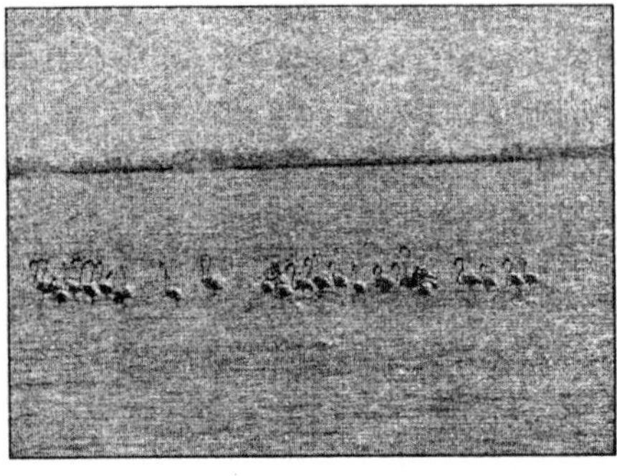

wigeon, common *Poachard* and common coot. The flamingo population whose number was less than 500 during last year increased their presence. A total number of 1624 greater flamingos were recorded during the census. Fifty-six lesser flamingos have also being counted during the census operation which were not available in Chilika lagoon during 2007 census. Rare birds such as *Palla's* fish eagle, Pintail snipe, Brahmin duck, Bar-headed geese, Oriental white ibis, *Euresian* spoon bill, etc were also recorded.

Hundred per cent increase in bird population in Nalabana island as compared to the previous year total can be attributed to de-weeding of *Salicornia* from the island, restoration of the habitat, construction of mounts etc which was supported by CDA. The continuous increase in bird population during last three years can also be attributed to the fact that the Chilika ecosystem has been maintained to cater the ecological and biological needs of different avian species coming from various countries of the northern hemisphere.

The bird's congregation in Chilika lagoon is the largest bird congregation in India where one can see the diversity of the migratory birds as well as the largest concentration over 15.5 sq.km area of Nalabana bird sanctuary.

Habitat Evaluation of Chilika Lagoon with Special Reference to Birds as Bio-indicators

The services of Bombay Natural History Society (BNHS) was commissioned with the following objectives:

(i) To assess the species-wise population of water flow and waders in different sectors of Chilika Lagoon and their relationship with habitat factors;

(ii) to study the population dynamics of migratory species using bird banding techniques;

(iii) to document the endangered, endemic and vulnerable species and their conservation needs;

(iv) to evaluate the impact of the restoration measures, especially opening of the new mouth;

(v) to suggest habitat improvement measures for Nalabana Island;

(vi) to enumerate the status of breeding birds and their conservation needs. BNHS commenced their study from December 2001.

They have also made a checklist of 211 numbers of birds from Chilika.

An innovative participatory micro watershed approach was envisaged for management of the catchments of the lagoon. The participatory approach adopted is a deviation from the conventional approach of implementing rather than facilitating. Watershed rehabilitation is conceived as a resource-based approach, with an objective to livelihood enhancement. The basic objective is to enable the community to prevent, arrest and reverse degradation of life support systems, particularly land and water, to produce biomass in a sustainable and equitable manner.

A micro-watershed known as Dengai Pahad, was undertaken on priority basis to demonstrate regeneration of the highly degraded ecosystem with emphasis on arresting silt load into the lagoon and sharing of benefits of water and land resources through community efforts. The area is ridded with poverty due to over use and abuse of natural resources and conflicts within community. Out of 19 tanks in the area 16 usually get dried up during summer, similarly several tube wells are defunct and water quality is deteriorated due to high concentration of iron in water. More than 50% of the agricultural land has been encroached upon and the grasslands are highly degraded due to soil erosion. This has lead to acute shortage of food, fuel and fodder contributing severely to the miseries of the local communities. Several activities undertaken through community efforts are briefly discussed in the article.

COMMUNITY PARTICIPATION

The PRA exercises were carried out to seek participation of the people. Efforts were made to revive old traditions and revitalize collective community spirit and to bring all primary stakeholders for planning of the natural resources management.

Watershed committees, user groups, self help groups and watershed volunteers were established to ensure the participation of the communities in the planning and implementation. Democratic procedures were followed in the selection of the office bearers and formulating regulations for the operation of these committees. Each village selected one educated youth as the volunteer for the watershed committee along with one women facilitator. The watershed committee applied to the District Administration for Registration of the Association under Societies Act 1860.

CONCLUSION

One of the major intervention was the distillation of the canal connecting the lagoon to the see and opening of the new mouth to restore the natural flows of water and salinity labels these resulted notably, in the improvement of the lagoon ecosystem with a phenomenal increases in the lagoons fish yield and the reduction of fresh water invasive species. The Chilika lagoon is a striking example of how restoration of the ecological characteristics of a site can result not only in improvement of the lagoon ecosystem but also immensely benefit the community depending on the wetland. The restoration of the Chilika lagoon derives its uniqueness from the strong participation of the local community, linkage with various National and International institution, intensive monitoring and assessment systems. The case of Chilika lagoon is a perfect example of how the listing of a site on the Montex Record can be used to promote majors to correct change in ecological character of a site, and to improve the socioeconomic condition of the population living in and around the site.

REFERENCES

Annandale, N. and S. Kemp. 1915. Fauna of the Chilika Lake. Introduction. *Mem.Indian Mus*. 5 (1): 1-120.

Banerjee, L.K and Anirban Roy, 2002. Plant Resources of Chilika lagoon. *Proc. International Workshop on Sustainable Development of Chilika lagoon,* 12-14 December, 1998 (Bhubaneswar): 168-171.

Banerjee, AC. and N.C. Roychoudhury. 1971. Observation on some Physico-chemical Features of the Chilika Lake. *Indian J. Fisheries*, 13 (1&2), July, 1971: 395-429. Blakford, W.T. 1872. *Sketch of Geology of Orissa,* GSI- Records, 5 part-2: 41.

Bhatta, K.S. and N.C.S. Samant. 1986. Crafts and Glars of Chilika Lagoon. National Conference of Natural Heritage Conservation. Berhampur (Orissa). *Abstr*. 18.

Bhatta, K.S. A.K. Pattnaik. & B.P. Behera. 2001. Further Contribution to the Fish Fauna of Chilika Lagoon, A Coastal Wetland of Orissa. *Geobios*., 28: 97 100.

Bhatta, K.S. and AK. Pattnaik. 2002 a. Environmental Monitoring of Chilika lagoon. *Proc. Int. nat. Workshop on Sustainable Development of Chilika Lagoon*. 12-14 December, 1998, Bhubaneswar (Orissa): 95-113.

Bhatta, K.S., R.N. Samal and AK. Pattnaik. 2002b. Impact of the New Mouth on the Salinity Progression of Chilika Lagoon. *Int.nat. Workshop on Restoration of Chilika Lagoon*. 18-20 January, 2002. Bhubaneswar (Orissa), Abstr: 6-7.

Bhatta, K.S., S.Mishra, AK. Pattnaik and S.K. Mohanty, 2004. Increase in Fisheries Output in Chilika Lagoon After Opening of the New Mouth. *Nat. Seminar on Responsible Fisheries and Aquaculture*, 12-13 February, 2004, Rangailunda (Berhampur), Orossa. Abstr: 74.

Bhatta, K. 1932. Algal Flora of Chilika Lake. *Mem. Asiat. Soc. Beng*. 11 (5) 165-198. 11.

Chaudhury, B. L. 1916 a. Description of Two New Species from Chilika Lake. Rec. India Mass., 12 (3): 105-108.

Chaudhury, B.L. 1916 b. Fauna of the Chilika Lake: Fish Part-1. *Mem. Indian Mus*., 5 (4): 403-440.

Chaudhury, B.L. 1916 c. Fauna of the Chilika Lake: Fish Part-II. *Mem. Indian Mus*., 5 (5) 441-458.

Chaudhury, B.L. 1917. Fauna of the Chilika Lake: Fish Part-III.*Mem. Indian Mus*., 5 (6) 491-508.

Chadhury, B.L. 1923. Fauna of the Chilika Lake: Fish Part IV. *Mem.Indian Mus*., 5 (II): 711-736.

CDA 2002. Collection and Estimation of Fish, Prawn and Crab Landings Statistics in the Chilika Lagoon: *Annual Report-2001-02*. Bull., 2: 45 p.

Devasundaram, M.P. 1951 a. Fishing Methods for Chilika Mullects. *Indian Fmg*., 12 (1-2): 22-25.

Devasundaram, M.P. 1951 b. Systematics of Chilika Mullets with a Key for Their Identification, *J. zool.Sr. India*., 3 (1) : 19-25.

Devasundaram, M.P. 1954. *A Report on the Fisheries of the Chilika Lake from 1548 to 1952*. Orissa Government Press, Cuttack.

Hora, S.L. 1923. Fauna of the Chilika Lake: Fish Part-V. *Mem. India Mus*., 5 (II): 737-769.

Hunter, W.W. 1872, Orissa. Smith Elder & Co., Waterloo place, London I: 17-80.

Jhingran, V.G. 1958. Observations on the Sea-ward Migration of Mugil Cephalus linnaeus from the Chilika Lake for Breeding. *Curr.Scl*., 27: 181-182.

Jhingran, V.G. 1959. On the Breeding Migration of Mugil Cephalus linnaeus from the Chilika Lake to the Sea. *Proc. India Sci. congr*, 46.

Jhingran, V.G.1963. *Report on the Fisheries of the Chilika Lake 1957-1960. Bull.* Cent. Inl. Fish. Res. Inst., Barrackpore (India).

Jhingran, V.G and AV. Natarajan. 1969. Study of the Fishery and Fish Populations of the Chilika Lake during the Period 1957-65. *J. Inland Fish. Sr. India.*, 1: 47-126.

Jhingran, V.G. and AV. Natarajan. 1968. Fisheries Resources of the Chilika Lake and is Bearing on Fisheries in Adjacent Areas of Bay of Bengal. Abstr. Symp. Living Resources of the Seas Around India. Cochin, 7-10 December. 1998, *Cent. Mar. Fish. Res. Inst. Maudapart camp*: 12.

Jhingran, V.G. and AV. Natarajan. 1969. Study of the Fishery Fish Populations of the Chilika Lake during the Period 1957-65. *J. Inland Fish. Sr. India.*, 1: 47-126.

Jones, S. and K.H. Sujansiaghani. 1951. The Hilsa Fishery of the Chilika Lake. B. *Bompay nat. Hist. Sr.*, 50(2) :264-280.

Jones, S. and K.H. Sujansiaghani. 1952. The Mani-jal of Chilika Lake: A Special Net for Biloniform Fish. *J. Bombay Nat. Hist. Soc.*, 51 (I): 288-289.

Jones, S. and K.H. Sujansinghani, 1954 Fish and Fisheries of Chilika Lake with Statistics of Fish Catches for the Years 1948-1950. *Indian J. Fish.*, (142): 256-344.

Kemp, S. 1915, Crustacea: Decapoda, Fauna of the Chilika Lake. *Mem. Indian Mus.*, 5: 199-325.

Koumans, F.P. 1941. Gobioid Fishes of India. *Mem.lndian Mus*, 13 (3): 205-313.

Kowtal, GV 1965. On the Breeding of Eleutheronema Tetratactylum (show) in the Chilika Lake. *Sci. & Cult.*, 31 (5): 262-263.

Kowtal, GV. 1970. A Note on the Early Development of Nematabora nasees (Bloch) _ from the Chilika Lake. *J. Inland Fish. Soc. India.*, 2: 152-155.

Kowtal, G.V. 1978. A Note on the Breeding and Ealy Development of pseu dosciaena coiber (Ham) from the Chilika Lake, *J.lnland Fish. Sr. India.*, 10: 152-155.

Menon, M.AS. 1961. On a Collection of Fish from Lake Chilika, Orissa. *Rec. Indian Mus.*, 59 (1&2): 41-69.

Mitra, G.N. 1946. *Development of the Chilika Lake*. Orissa Government Press, Cuttack.

Mitra, G.N. and M.P. Devasundaram. 1954. On the Hilsa of the Chilika Lake with a note on the Occurrence of the Hisla in Orissa. *J.Asiatic. Sr. Sci.*, 20 (1):33-40.

Mitra, G.N. and P. Mohapatra. 1957, *Bulletin on the Development of Chilika Lake Survey Report on the Fishing Industry*. Government Press, Cuttack.

Mohapatra, P. 1955. The Thatta-konda-A Screen Trap of the Chilika Lake. J. Bombay nat. Hist. Soc., 53: 277-279.

Mohanty, S.K. 1971. Preliminary Observations on Induced Spawning of Mugil Cephalus in the Chilika Lake. *J. Indian Fish. Assoc.*, 1 (2): 1-7.

Mohanty, S.K. 1973. Further Additions to the Fish Fauna of the Chilika lake. *J. Bombay nat. Hist. Soc.*, 72 (3) 863-866.

Mohanty, S.K. 1975 a. The Breeding of Economist Fishes of the Chilika Lake-6. Review. *Bull. Deptt. Mar. Sc. Univ. Cochin.*, 7 (2): 543-559.

Mohanty, S.K. 1975 b. On the Food of Bagda, Penaeus Monodon Fabricius from the Chilka Lake. *Bull. Deptt. Mar.Sc. Univ. Cochin.*, 7 (3): 645-652.

Mohanty, S.K. 1975 c. Further Observations on the Crab Landings in the Chilika Lake during 1973. *Bull.Deptt. Mar. Sc. Univ. Coachin.*, 7 (3): 631-635.

Mohanty, S.K. d. Some Observations on the Physico-chemical Featuers of the Outer Channel of the Chilika Lake during 1971-73. *Bull. Deptt. Mar. Sc. Univ. Coachin.* 7(2): 69-89.

Mohanty, S.K. 1973. Notes on Crab Landings in the Chilika Lake during 1971 and 1972. Cent, Institute Fish Educ., *Bombay Recr. Club Sour.*: 1-3.

Mohanty, S.K. 1978. Prawn Fishery of Chilika Lake: Its Contribution to the Export Trade of Marine Products of Orissa. *Seaford Export J.* 10 (2): 1-4.

Mohanty, S.K. 2001 Sustainable Fisheries Management in Chilika Lagoon. Presented at the National Workshop on Sustainable Development and Biodiversity Conservation in Chilika Lagoon, Bhubaneswar 9-10 February (2001).

Mohanty, S.K. 1988. Rational Utilization of Brakishwater Resources of the Chilika Lagoon for Aquaculture. Chilika, the Pride of our Wetland Heritage. *Orissa Env. Soc.* (1988):36-39.

Mohanty, S.K. 2002. Fisheries Biodiversity of Chilika Lagoon. *Chilika Newsletter*. January (2002)., 3: 11-12.

Mohanty, S.K., AK. Pattnaik, K.S. Bhatta and Rajeeb K. Mohanty. 2002. Fisheries Resources of Chilika lagoon: An Overview. Presented at the International Workshop on Restoration of Chilika lagoon. Bhubaneswar (18-20 January, 2002. Abstr: 17-18.

Mohanty, S.K. Rajeeb K. Mohanty and H.S. Badapanda. 2001. Fishery Dynamics and Management of the Chilika lagoon. *Fishing chimes.*, 22 (5): 42-43.

Mohanty, S.K. 2003. Evaluation of Commercial Fish Landings from Chilika Lagoon Before and After Hydrological Intervention. *Chilika Newsletter*, 4: 20-21.

Mohanty, S.K. , KS. Bhatta, S. Mishra and A Mohapatra 2004. Fisheries Enhancement after Hydrological Intervention in Chilika Lagoon and Strategies for Responsible Management Presented at the National Seminar on Responsbile Fisheries and Aquaculture. 12-13 February, 2004, Rangailunda (Berhampur) Abstr: 70.

Mohanty, Rajeeb K. and S.K. Mohanty. 2002. Factors Affecting Fishes and Shell Fish Biodiversity in Chilika Lagoon. *Fishing Chimps*, 22 (5): 42-43.

Mohanty, N.D and G. Behera, 2002. Studies on Shifting of inlet, Variations of Water Level and Its Effect on Salinity Concentrations of Chilika Lagoon. Proc. International Workshop on Sustainable Development of Chilika Lagoon, Bhubaneswar, 12-14 Dec. 1948: 48-59.

Mohanty, H.F. 1950 *Supplement to the Botany of Bihar and Orissa*. Catholic Press, Ranchi.

Mohapatra A E, Rajeeb K. Mohanty A E, S. K. Mohanty A E, K.S. Bhatta A E, N.R. Das Received: 6 March 2006/Accepted: 12 November 2006/ Published online: 13 January 2007, Springer Science+Business Media B.V. 2007.

Nayak, B.U. L.K. Ghosh, S.K. Roy and R.S. Kankara. 2002. A Study on Hydrodynamics and Salinity in the Chilika Lagoon. Proc. International Workshop on Sustainable Development of Chilika Lagoon Bhubaneswar, 12-14 December, 1998: 31-47.

Pattnaik, S. 1971 Seasonal Abundance and Distribution of Bottom Fauna of the Chilika Lake. *J. mar. biol. Ass. India*, 1971, 13 (I): 106-125.

Pattnaik, S. 1973 a. Observations on the Seasonal Fluctuations of Plankton in the Chilika Lake. *India J. Fish*, 20: 43-55.

Pattnaik, S. 1973 b. A Study of the Aquatic Plants of Chilika Lake. Proc. Nat. Acad. Sci. India., 43 (b): 53-65.

Pattnaik, S. 1980, Distribution and Abundance of Large Aquatic Plants in Chilika Lagoon. In : Summer Institute on Brackishwater Capture and Culture Fisheries. CIFRI, Barrackpore, WB: 1-7.

Pattnaik, AK 2000. Conservation of Chilika: An Overview. *Chilika Newsletter*, 1 July, 2000: 3-5.

Pattnaik, AK. 2001. Hydrological Intevention for Restoration of Chilika Lagoon. *Chilika Newsletter*, 2, May, 2001.

Pattnaik, AK 2002. Participatory Approaches for Biodiversity Conservation of Chilika Lagoon. *Chilika Newsletter*, 3 Janauary, 2002: 5-7.

Pattnaik, AK 2002. Chilika Lake: An Overview. Proc. International *Workshop on Sustainable Development of Chilika lagoon*; Bhubaneswar 12-14, 1998: 12-19.

Pattnaik, AK 2003. Rejuvenation of Chilika Lagoon: A Journey from Montreux Record to Ramsar Wetland Conservation Award. *Chilika Newsletter*, 4. December 2003: 2-3.

Panigrahy, R.C. 2002. Environmental Aspects of the Chilika Lagoon: A Sensitive Coastal Ecosystem of Orissa. *Proc. International Workshop on Sustainable Development of Chilika Lagoon*, Bhubaneswar 12-14, December, 1998: 60-76.

Panda, P.C. and S.N. Pattnaik, 2002. An Enumeration of the Flowering Plants of Chilika Lagoon and Its Immediate Neighbourhood. *Proc. International Workshop on Sustainable Development of Chilika Lagoon*, Bhubaneswar 12-14 December, 1998: 122-141.

Panda, P.C., A.K. Pattnaik, J. Rath and S.N. Pattnaik. 2002. Flora of Chilika Lake and Its Immediate Neighbourhood: A Check list. *J. Eco. Taxon. Bot.*, 26 (1): 1-20.

Rattnaik, S. 1970. A Contribution to the Fishery and Biology of the Chilika "Sahal" (EleTheronema tetra dactyllun). proc. Indian Nat. Sci. Acad., 36B (I): 33-61.

Roy, J. C and N. Sahoo. 1957. Additions to the Fish Fauna of the Chilika Lake. J. *Bombay nat. Hist. Soc.*, 54 :943-953.

Rajan, S. 1964. Environmental studies of the Chilika Lake: Feeding Spectrum of Fishes. *Indian J. Fish.*, 2: 421-532.

Ramanadham, R, M.P.M. Reddy and A.V.S. Murty. 1964. Limnology of the Chilika Lake, *J. Mar. bial. Ass. India.*, 6 (2): 183-201.

Rama Rao, K.V. 1995. *Pisces. In: Fauna of the Chilika Lake.* ZSI : 483-506.

Rajan, S.S. Pattnaik and N.C. Basu. 1968. New Records of Fishes from Chilika Lake. *J.Zool.Soc. India.*, 20 (I) : 80-83.

Roy, J.C. 1954. Periodicity of the Plankton Diatoms of the Chilika Lake for the Years 1950-1951. *J. Bombaynat. Hist. Soc.*, 52 (I) 112-123.

Roy, J.C. and N. Sahoo. 1957. Additions to the Fish Fauna of the Chilika Lake. J. *Bombay nat. Hist. Soc.*, 54: 943-953.

Smal, R.C. 1992. Remote Sensing Studies in Geomorphology of Chilika Lagoon in Orissa. In: R.L. Karak (Ed.) *Natural Resources Management: A New Perspective*. NNRMS, ISRO Hqr. Banglore: 417-423.

Samal, RC. 1993. Remote Sensing Study on Geomorphic and Sedimentologic Evolution of the Coastal Tract Between Dharma and Palur, Orissa, India (Un Published Ph.D. Thesis), Utkal University, Vanivihar, BBSR.

Samal, RC. 2002. Environmental Geomorphology of Chilika Lagoon Orissa, Proc. *International Workshop on sustainable Development of Chilika Lagoon*, Bhubaneswar 12-14 December, 1998: 246-259.

Venkatarathnam, K. 1970. Formation of the Barrier Spit and Other Sand Ridges Near Chilika Lake in East Coast of India. Marine Geo., 9: 101.

6

Observations on Susceptibility Index of *Drosophila melanogaster* to Synthetic Pyrethroid Insecticide

S.A. Choudhary[1]

ABSTRACT

A Synthetic Pyrethroid (Fenvalerate) was analysed for its toxic effects on *Drosophila Melanogaster*. It has been estimated that LC_{50} was 0.007µl/100ml food. These studies revealed that fenvalerate is toxic as it had a pronounced effect on the rate of development, fecundity and viability of *Drosophila melanogaster*.

INTRODUCTION

The synthetic insecticides or pesticides are biodegradable with low, mammalian toxicity and hence these pesticides have gained much more importance and now these are widely being used to manage several categories of pests. *Drosophila* has been reported as tomato fields pest by Peeper *et al.* (1955) and Michelbacher and Middlekauff (1954). The eggs are oviposited

1. Department of Zoology, Government P.G College, Rajouri (J&K).

on the damaged parts or cracks of the tomatoes thus leading to the problem of food contamination. Efforts to relive this problem, the fenvalerate (20% active ingredient of synthetic pyrethroid) were chosen because of its broad spectrum activity.

A review of literature reveals that many pesticides and insecticides have been used against this test-insect, such as Rani *et al.* (1977), Basheer *et al.* (1999), Akhter *et al.* (2001), Akhter (2002), Choudhary (2002) and Razdan and Rana (2002). However, fenvalerate has been used on this test-insect and hence the present study was undertaken to observe toxicity of fenvalerate on developmental rate, fecundity and viability of *Drosophila melanogaster.*

MATERIAL AND METHODS

A pure strain of *Drosophila melanogaster* was obtained from *Drosophila* Stock, Centre, School of Life Sciences, Devi Ahilya Vishwavidalaya, Indore. The pure culture was maintained under the laboratory conditions at a temperature 25±5° C and used for experiment after 5-6 generations when they were fully acclimatized. The culture was fed on a standard food medium consisting of corn flour 17g, agar 2g, sugar 12g, yeast 3g, nepagin 19, propionic acid 1 ml, 70% alcohol 1 ml and distilled water 360 ml (for 10 experimental bottles) which was prepared according to the method described by Aijaz *et al.* (1987).

The LC_{50} (0.077µl/100 ml food) was calculated first and then a sub-lethal dose (0.007µl/100 ml food) was selected and mixed. in the culture medium according to the method described by Dhingra *et al.* (1988) in order to determine the effectiveness of the test compound.

The different cross combinations: (i) T♀ x U♂ (ii) T♀ x T♂, and (iii) U♀ x T♂, were formed and examined against the control set bottles (U♀ x U♂) [T = treated, U = untreated]. Files were etherized for separation of males and females in ratio of 1: 1 and were then transferred in the culture bottles (*vide supra*). They were allowed to mate and lay eggs.

Eggs were collected by Delcour procedure (Delcour, 1969). Eggs of each set were allowed to undergo (hatching) development in the same culture bottles and observation was thus made to find out the effect on fecundity, development rate and viability.

The developmental rate and the flies emerged were also counted and sexed every day from the first day up to the last day of eclosion. The collected data were analyzed statistically by log-dose/probit regression line method (Finney, 1971). The statistical calculation of mean, standard deviation and standard error were based on the biological statistics by Fisher and Yates 1963). The test of significance was made using simple t-test.

RESULTS AND DISCUSSION

In the cross-combinations either male or female or both were treated with fenvalerate, egg laying was delayed by 9-18 days as compared to control. This may be due to inhibitory effects of compound on gonadal development. Razdan (2002) observed a significant fall in oviposition in mutant *Drosophila melanogaster* with the cypermethrin treatment. The range and average hatch of successive egg batches laid by the flies treated with fenvalerate have been depicted in Table 6.1. Among the laid eggs a few egg batches did not hatch completely due to either lack of vitelline for normal embryo growth or possibly some deleterious effects of fenvalerate on embryogenesis. This finding is in complete agreement with that of Choudhary (2003). The treated flies showed that laid eggs as 298, 284, and 321 in the cross combinations of (i) T♀ x U♂, (ii) T♀ x T♂, and (iii) U♀ x T♂, respectively showing that fenvalerate was more effective when both the sexes were treated.

The possible explanation may be high metabolic activity and rate of excretion in both the treated flies (T♀ x T♂) than males (U♀ x T♂) or females (T♀ x U♂) treated flies but the effect of given insecticide was also induced in cross combinations where only males were treated may be due to transfer of compound from males to females during copulation (Brokovec 1979).

Table 6.1: Mean development time of *Drosophila melanogaster* after fenvalerate intoxication

Nature of cross	*Mean development time*		
	Group	*Males*	*Females*
T♀ x U♂	20.33 ±0.89	14.03 ±2.20	18.04 ±2.02
T♀ x T♂	26.75 ±2.07	16.08 ±2.05	20.33 ±0.02
U♀ x T♂	16.66±1.63	13.66 ±0.03	15.05 ±1.34
U♀ x U♂	11.51 ±0.07	11. 54 ±0.11	11.34 ± 0.21

The cause for inability of eggs to hatch might be due to chitin synthesis inhabiting properties of fenvalerate (Post and Mulder, 1974). As the cuticle and mouth hooks are chintinous in nature whose development start during embryogenesis and is completed before egg hatch, it is possible that fenvalerate, in the present study has penetrated into eggs and interfered with development of cuticle and mouth hooks, rendering them less rigid and incapable of providing sufficient supports to the muscles, depriving the larvae of a method to come out of embryonic envelops as the dipteran larvae use body muscles and mouth aperture to rapture the vitelline membrane and chorion to escape eclosion (Poulson, 1950). The significant mortalities were observed in successive instars (L1, L2 and L3) due to fenvalerate is the interference, in the synthesis of chiten during moulting of larvae in successive instars in to pre-pupae. The new malformed cuticle cannot give sufficient support to the muscles involved in ecdysis, which results in inability to cast the exuviae and partially free themselves but finally loose moisture,'turn black and die (Van Daalen *et al.*, 1972; Wellinga *et al.*, 1973).

A significant lengthening *of* developmental time is a fairly good indication *of* somatic effects caused by the chemical in test substrate. The present findings support the view *of* Lunning (1966) using sodium salicylate and other compounds, Sorsa and Pfeifer (1973a and b) using certain oragnomercurials and cadmium chloride and Vasudev and Krishnamurthy (1982-83) using Dithame M-45, observed similar effects. Other environmental factors such as crowding have been demonstrated to have an effect on the rate of development. The relative developmental time has been prolonged in crowded conditions, in different species of *Drosophila* (Krishnamurthy *et al*., 1993). Thus it can be said that any viability in the environment is having profound influence on the rate *of* development. It is concluded that chemical environment is responsible for increased developmental time in the treated batches. As has been shown, the rate *of* development, the males and the females exhibit the different sensitivity in each treated sets due to the female were more sensitive than males (Vasudev & Krishnamurthy, 1979).

It has been observed that the viability reduced more in treated batches as compare to the control due to mortality occur mostly during the larval stages and that the first instarlarvae are the most sensitive to the given insecticides. On the observation to the pupae *of Drosophila melanogaster*, a significant fall in adult emergence has been recorded in all treated batches which were depicted in Table 6.2. Most of the adults of both the sexes were either died within the puparium or died 12 hours after emergence from the puparium due to the emerged adults (males and females) was abnormal with white body, emerged forcibly by insecticidal. The abnormal adults were unable to cast of the puparium completely and the structure appears between pupae and adult died within two days of their partial emergence.

Less number of male adults was also recorded as compare to the females in treated batches. The reason for differential sexual emergence may be attributed to the different size of males and females. Hence, consequences of the application of' fenvalerate on fecundity, rate of development and viability of adult emergence resulted in the suppression of population growth. The effect of given synthetic insecticide was assessed in each set (Table 6.3) on the basis of susceptibility index (Chaudhary, 2002 and Akhter, 1999).

Table 6.2: Effect of fenvalerate in fecundity and viability of *Drosphila melanogaster*

Treated sets	*No. of eggs laid*	*No. of males and females emerged out of eggs laid*		*Total No. of adults emerged*	*% viability*
		Males	*Females*		
T♀ x U♂	298.33	45	65	110	34.52*
T♀ x T♂	284.66	34	56	90	29.86*
U♀ x T♂	307.66	57	70	127	40.62*
U♀ x U♂	321.66	154	156	310	96.37*

* Statistically significant at 5% level of significance.

Table 6.3: Susceptibility of *Drosophila melanogaster* to insecticide (Fenvalerate) intoxication

Sets	*No. of Sets*	*Developmental period in days*	*Adults emergence*	*Susceptibility Index*
T♀ x U♂	3	20.33	110	76.88
T♀ x T♂	3	26.75	90	83.18
U♀ x T♂	3	16.66	127	70.93
U♀ x U♂	3	11.51	310	50.17

REFERENCES

Aijaz, R.; Samad, P.; Khan, M.F. and Baig, M.M.H. 1987. Evaluation of Best and Cheapest Artificial Diet for the *Drosophila Melanogaster*. *Pak. J. Zool.* 19(3): 302-306.

Akhter, S. 1999. Susceptibility Index of Fenvalerate to the Mutant Forms of *Drosophila Melanogaster*. M. Phil Dissertation, Dr. B.R. Ambedkar University, Agra; 105-107.

Akhter, S.; Bahadur, R. R. and Verma, R. K. 2001. Toxicity of Different Formulation of Fenvalerate 20EC Against Different Mutant Forms of *Drosophila melanogaster* (Meigen). *J. Agri.* Sci. *Res.* 37 (1&2): 75-77.

Akhter, S. 2002. Selective Toxicity of Fenvalerate (Synthetic Pyrethroid) on the Fecundity and Hatchability of Laboratory Selected Population of Mutant form (Yellow) of *Drosophila melanogaster* (Meigen). *Int. J. Mendel,* 19(3) : 117-118.

Basheer, S.; Vasudev, V.; Venu, R.; Guruprasad, K.P. and Harish, K. P. 1999. Toxic Effect of a Recently Introduced Carbamate Pesticides, Dunet (methomyl) on *Drosophila melanogaster, J. Environ. Biol.* 20 (2): 135-139.

Borkovec, A. 1979. Insect Reproduction Suppression by Inhibitors of Chitin Synthesis. *Proc. 2nd Internal Symp Invertebrate Reprod.* Dayis, Ca, Aug.: 1-4.

Choudhary, S. 2002. Relative Susceptibility of Mutant form (Sepia) of *Drosophila melanogaster* to Synthetic Pyrethroid (fenvalerate). *Proc. Zool. Soc. India.* 1(1&2): 43-45.

Choudhary, S. 2003. Toxic Effects of Fenvalerate on Fecundity and Hatchability of Mutant forms of *Drosophila melanogaster* (Meigen). *Geobios,* 30 (2-3): 203-204.

Delcour, L. 1969. A Rapid and Efficient Method of Egg Collecting. *DIS.* 44: 133-134.

Dhingra, G.B.; Chaudhary, J. B. and Sareen, P.K. 1988. Genotoxic Effects of a Synthetic Pyrethroid Insecticide on *Drosophila. Drosophila Infor. Serve.* 67: 27.

Finney, D.J. 1971. *Probit Analysis,* Cambridge University Press p. 303.

Fisher, R.A. and Yates, Y. 1963. *Statistical Tables for Biological Agriculture and Medical Research.* Longman 6th ed: 146.

Krishnamurthy, N.B.; Nagaraj, H.J. and Vasudev, V. 1993. Pre-Adult Competition Studies in Three Sympatric Species of *Drosophila. Bio. Zent. Bl.* 112: 300-311.

Lunning, K.G. 1966. *Drosophila* Test in Pharmacology. *Nature,* 209: 84-86.

Michelbacher, A. E. and Middlekauff, W. S. 1954. Vinegar Fly Investigation in Northern California. J. *Econ. Entomol.* 42: 917-922.

Peeper, B.B; Reed, J. D. and Starnes, O.1955. *Drosophila* as a Pest of Processing Tomatoes. *New Jersey Agr. Sta. ento. Bull.* 266: 8.

Post, L. C. and Mulder, R. 1974. Insecticidal Properties and Mode of Action of 1 (2, 6-dihalogenbenzoyl) - 3- Phenyl Urea. Am. *Chem. Soc. Symp.* Ser. 2: 136-143.

Poulson, D.F., 1950. Histogenesis, Oryanogensis and Differentiation in the Embryo of *Drosophila melanogasler* Meigen. In: *Biology of Drosophila,* John Wiley and Son. Inc. New York. 168-174.

Rani, S; Tabassum, R, Naqvi, S.N.H, Ahmed. J, Sultan, B. and Khan, M.F. 1997. Comparative Toxicity of Different Formulations of Cypermethrin, Deltamethrin and Permethrin Against *Drosophila melanogaster* (K.U. Strain). *J. Environ. Biol.* 18 (4): 343-349.

Razdan, T. 2002. Effect of Cypermethrin on the Fecundity of Mutant *Drosophila Melanogaster. Poll. Res.* 21(2): 175-176.

Razdan, T. and Rana. K.S. 2002. Effect of Cybil on the Growth and Development of *Drosophila melanogaster* (Meigen). *Geobios,* 29: 200.

Sorsa, M. and Pfeifer, S. 1973a. Response of Puffing Pattern to in vivo Treatments with Organo-mercurials in *Drosophila melanogaster. Hereditas,* 74: 89-102.

Sorsa, M. and Pfeifer. S. 1973b. Response of Puffing Pattern to in vivo Treatments with Organo-mcrcurials in *Drosophila melanogaster Hereditas,* 75: 273-277.

Van Daalen, J. J.; Meltzer, J.; Mulder, R. and Wellinga, K. 1972. A Selective Insecticide with a Noval Mode of Action. *Naturewise,* 59: 312-313.

Vasudev,. V. and Krishnamurthy,. N. B. 1982-83. Effect of Dithane, M-45 on the Rate of Development, Viability, Morphology and Fecundity in *Drosophila melanogaster. J. Mys. Univ.* 29: 79-86.

Vasudev, V. and Krishnamurthy, N.B. 1979. Effect of a Lead Compound on Rate of Development and Viability in *Drosophila Melanogaster. Ind. J Heredity.* 11: 63-66.

Wellinga, K., Mulder, R. and Van Daalen, J.J. 1973. Synthesis and Laboratory Evolution of 1-(2.6- Disubstituted benzol) -3 phenylureas. A New Class of Insecticide I. 1 (2, 6-dicholorobenzoyl)-3-phenylureas. *J. Agric. Food Chem.* 21: 348-345.

7

The Application of Biopesticides (Natural Pesticides) is Basic Need to Save Ecology and Environment

Deepali[1]
Kamal Kishor Gangwar[1]

ABSTRACT

India is a fast developing country and land of agriculture. About 70% populations are depending on agriculture, so the farmers used uninterrupted indiscriminate conventional pesticide to accomplish the demand of increasing population. The use of this chemical pesticide for a long period of time, many harmful insects and pests has developed resistant against chemical pesticides. In this article an attempt have been made to implicate and promote the application of biopesticide at place of chemical pesticide. There are certain fungi, bacteria, viruses and plants species which have unique properties to provide us

1. Department of Zoology and Environmental Science, Faculty of Life Sciences, Gurukul Kangri University, Haridwar-249 404.
E-mail: deepali.phd@rediffmail.com

natural products, which can be used against to control the insect and pests with secure environment.

INTRODUCTION

A pesticide is eco-friendly only if it does not pollute to environment and does not affect the health of living beings directly or indirectly (even a sub-chronic and sub lethal doses).

To have better produces a country has to depend upon the uses of pesticides. But the continuous use of chemical pesticides beyond the permissible limit may have negative effect on human health as well as environment because of their toxic potential.

Indiscriminate use of pesticides over the years has result many problems caused by their interaction with biological system. The enormous and continued use of pesticides has added to the environmental pollution to such an extent that human health is adversely affected. Some times, pesticide such as DDT, DDE, BHC, Methyl mercury etc. are transferred through the food chain and accumulated in the body of living organisms. This phenomenon is called bio-magnification. They show various dangerous side effects and many harmful insects become resulted to these chemical pesticides.

Another problem that occurs with organic pesticides is biotransformation. In this phenomenon some times several compounds when administered in the body convert nontoxic form into highly toxic one. Some times DDT converts into DDE which is highly toxic. This reaction occurs in higher organisms having specialized enzyme systems.

A novel approach toward development of eco-friendly pesticides is to develop new bio-pesticides from micro-organism or plants, which should be apparently or non apparently, non toxic.

BACTERIA AS BIOPESTICIDES

Bacillus thuringiensis (Bt)

Bacterium *B. thuringiensis* is widely distributed. It can be isolated from soils, litters and dead insects (pathogenic to larvae of lepidoptera). It is a spore forming bacterium and damage larvae after ingestion of spores by secreting a single large crystal in the cell at opposite end during sporulation. Crystals (toxin) are protenaceous and insecticidal in nature. Although, crystals with activities on other invertebrates and crystals having no detected biological activity have also been reported (Lecadet *et al.*, 1999). Several *B.thuringiensis* insecticidal crystals protein (ICPs) has been developed and commercialized sprayble biopesticides and transgenic plant incorporated protectants for agricultural applications. *Bacillus thuringiensis* crystal proteins of the Cry 34 and Cry 35 classes function as binary toxins showing activity on the western corn rootworm, *Diabrotica virgifera virgifera* Le Conte. (Schnept *et al.*, 2005).

Transgenic *Bt* cotton as currently commercialized in India, incorporates a Cry 1 AC gene derived from the soil bacterium *Bacillus thuringiensis*. The gene expresses a crystal protein deta endo toxin called Cry 1 AC in all parts of the transgenic plants. The protein is toxic to many lepidopteran caterpillars that feed on the transgenic plants (Kranthi *et al.*, 2005a). The Cry 1 AC content in seeds was found to be 1.77±0.23 mg/g and the variability b/w individual seed and seed lots was minimal. Bioassay on *Helicoverpa armigera* using *Bt*-seeds stored at room temperature for two years showed that there was no significant reduction in bioactivity of the toxin present in the seeds (Kranthi *et al.*, 2005a). The Cry 1AC expression was found to be variable among the hybrids and also between different plant parts. The leaves of Bt-cotton plants were found to have the highest levels of Cry 1AC expression followed by squares, bolls and flowers. Increasing levels of *Helicoverpa armigera* survival were correlated with the toxin levels decreasing below 1.80 mg/g in the plants parts.(Kranthi *et al.*,2005b). Cry 1AC expression decreased consistently as the plant aged. (Kranthi *et al.*, 2005b).

Baseline susceptibility of larvae of the American bollworm, *Helicoverpa armigera* (Hubner) to *Bacillus thuringiensis* Berl Var. Kurstaki was studied by a diet incorporation method ninety six hour median lethal hour (LC_{50}) *bt var* Kurstaki strains parasporal crystal toxins varied widely for neonate larvae of different insect populations from nine locations in India showed differences in their susceptibility to *bt var* Kurstaki strains and individual Cry toxins viz. Cry 1Aa 10.5, Cry 1Ab 12.8, Cry 1Ac 16.2, HD-114.1 and HD^{-73} 5.7-fold. (Chandrashekar *et al.*, 2005).

Insect populations obtained from pigeon pea crops at Navsari from December 2000 to January 2001 and at Delhi from October 1998 to November 2000 should temporal variation in their susceptibility to Bt var kurstaki HD-1 and HD-73. (Chandrashekar *et al.*, 2005).

Pseudomonas Fluorescence

It has been observed that some rhizospheric bacteria have biocontrol capabilities. They produce some nematicidal metabolites i.e. 2° metabolite 2, 4-diacetyl phloroglucinol (DAPG) by many fluorescent *pseudomonas species h*as been found to play a major role in the biocontrol to plant parasitic nematodes including potato cyst nematode (Cronin *et al.*, 1997) and the root knot nematodes meloidogyne species (Siddiqui and Shaukat, 2003 a, b).

Streptomyces Species

Recent studies on marine micro-organisms have focused mainly on the discovery of human drugs, but rare information about marine micro algae possessing insecticidal activities has been reported.

The isolated Streptomyces species, 173 has great insecticidal potency. This work indicated that marine micro organism could be an important source of insecticidal antibiotics and the improved antibrine shrimp bioassay is suitable for primary screening. According to Xiong *et al.*, (2004), total 331 isolates were examined through bioassay of brine shrimp and 40 isolates (12.08%) showed potential insecticidal activities. Of the 40 isolates one isolates, designated streptomyces species, 173 was found to have strong insecticidal activity against both brine shrimp and *Helicoverpa armigera* similar to that of avermectin B1.

FUNGI AS BIOPESTICIDES

Chromolaena odorata commonly known eupatium, is an alien, obnoxious and aggressive weed. It suppresses young plantations, agricultural crops and smothers vegetation, as it possesses allelopathic potentialities and growth inhibitors. (Ambica and Jayachandra, 1980)

A field survey was conducted in agriculture and forest areas of Eupaterium endemic districts in Karnataka. The survey resulted in isolation of 18 different isolates distributed in nine different genera. All organisms were foliar pathogens except *A .pullulan* which was a floral pathogen. All the isolates satisfied Koch's postulates and hence proved to be pathogenic to the weeds. (Prashanthi and Kulkarni, 2005).

Trichoderma as Biopesticides

In India, all pulses and oil seed crops are affected by many diseases of which the root rot disease caused by the fungi *Macrophomina phaseolina* results in 20-30% loss of produce worth million of rupees. The biocontrol agent *Trichoderma viridae*, a fungus effectively checks the spread of root rot disease of pulses and oil seeds. Seed treatment with the product of this bioagent is more effective than the conventional fungicides. Further, the bioagent is able to survive and multiply at the root zone of the crops. The product is used at the rate of 4.0 g/kg of seeds of crops like groundnut, chickpea, sunflower, sesamum, black gram, green gram and cotton (Jayaraj, 1994).

PARASITOIDS AS BIOPESTICIDES

The egg parasitoids, Trichogramma species can be mass produced even under rural situations for effective management of sugarcane internode borer. It attacks the egg stage of the pests. It can also be released in cotton against bollworms. It efficiency has been shown in more than 3000 ha in many districts of Tamil Nadu against sugarcane borer. The loss due to the pest in sugar cane varies from 12-18%. Bollworm in cotton account for a total loss of 15% of lint production. It is mass production of laboratory host insect viz., egg of rice moth *Corcyra cephaloneca,* which is in turn cultured on broken grains of pearl millets or sorghum in plastic trays. The eggs of this stored product insect are collected in large quantities and exposed to parasitoid by pasting on paper cards. The parasitized cards are taken to sugarcane fields and tied on leaves at 2.5 cc/ha/release. There is a greate scope and demand for this parasitoids against sugarcane and cotton pests. Sugarcane is grown in 33 lakh ha. and cotton in 73 lakh ha in India (Jayaraj, 1994).

VIRUSES AS BIOPESTICIDES

Viruses can be multiply under laboratory condition on the host insects and then be released in to the crops to control the pests. The viruses are species specific and do not affect to other species.

Viruses from two groups i.e. NPVs and CPVs, are used as biocontrol agent, which are as following:

Nuclear Polyhedrosis Viruses (NPVs)

In case of *Heliothis armigera,* the Tamil Nadu G.D. Naidu Agricultural University has succeeded in developing a technique for mass production of a virus called Nuclear Polyhedrosis Virus (NPV). The NPVs of *H. armigera* as well as *Spodeptera litura* are naturally occurring and the strains isolated indigenously have been found to be quite effective in the field control of pests. The efficacy of viruses in the control of the pests on crops such as cotton, pulses, tobacco, groundnut, sunflower and vegetables has also been demonstrated in the farmer's fields. Unfortunately there is no commercial organization producing these viral insecticides in India to meet the demand of the farmers. It is anticipated that based on the recent developments there will be a very high demands for viral biopesticides for the management o f *H. armigera* and *S. litura*. The total expenditure for each unit will be Rs. 8.90 lakhs, which is expected to bring a net profit of Rs. 1.03 lakhs.

To produce the viruses in the Tamil Nadu, on a mass scale, the host insect has to be reared in the laboratory. *Heliothis armigera* can be reared on a semi synthetic diet.

The larvae from the insect culture are separated and allowed in the same synthetic diet. The virus is inoculated and the virosed larvae can be seen in 3-5 days (Yojana,1992).

The disease symptoms include decrease in feeding, restlessness, body becoming soft and pliable, developing a pinkish white color on the ventral surface followed by death. The dead larvae are collected and kept in distilled water for one week for purification. They are then ground in a grinder and the virus is isolated. Virus suspension of known concentration mixed with pure water is sprayed in the field to kill *Heliothis armigera*. This has proved to be very successful.

Cytoplasmic Polyhedrosis Viruses (CPVs)

The CPVs which are present in more than 200 insects, out of which only a few have been used for control of insect pests. For the first time in France, a CPV of pine precessionary caterpillar (*Thaumetopoea pityocamps*) was applied as pesticides used for the control of pine forest pests. In 1974, Japan produced a commercial preparation of CPVs under the name 'Matsukemin' for the control of a pine caterpillar (*Dendrolimus spectabilis*). This insect was controlled fully upon application of 10" polyhedral inclusion bodies per hectare.

PLANT PESTICIDES

Plant products have been used as pesticides or insecticides since ancient times in every part of country. Their use was common in the rural and tribal areas and can be still observed. Plant synthesizes many chemicals in addition to their food material exclusively for self-defense against pest and diseases. Plant insecticides have low mammalian toxicity. Chinese were the first to discover the value of Derris (*Derris elliptica* and *Derris malaccenisis*) as an effective insecticide. Plant pesticides have some characteristics:

- Easy availability.
- Preparation should be simple.
- It should not be time consuming.
- Highly selective or target species with little toxicity towards non target organisms and environment.

Plant insecticides can be categorized as follows:

(i) Primary Toxicants, e.g. nicotine, rotenone, etc.

(ii) Essential Oils, e.g. oil of citronella, lemon grass and cassia).

(iii) Fixed Oils e.g. cotton seed oil and fish oil.

(iv) Miscellaneous.

PRIMARY TOXICANTS

Indian Neem (*Azadirachta indica*)

Indians commonly use it due to insecticidal and medicinal properties. All parts of neem tree possess insecticidal activity but seed kernel is most active. Entomologists have found that neem materials can affect more than 200 insects' species as well as some mites, nematodes, fungi and bacteria. Neem bark, leaf, fruit and oil as well as extracts with in various solvents especially, ethanol have been found to exhibit insecticidal activity.

Azadirachtin, a tetranortriterpenoid from *Azadirachta indicia, A.juss.*(Meliaceae), is well-known as an insect growth inhibitor (*Rembold et al.*, 1982).

Source of Azadirachtin is leaves and berries of *Azadirachta indicia* and Melia azedarach (Chines berry tree). It inhibits the feeding and growth of insects belonging to several texa. Although its effects involves intervention in endocrinal activities (Barnby and Klocke, 1990). Azadirachtin has three pronged action on insects. It is a growth inhibitor, preventing the growth of insects from one stage of their life cycle to another. Eggs do not hatch into larvae and larvae do not becomes adults. As it is an antifecdant, insects that come in contact, stop feeding and die of starvation. And thirdly, azadirachtin repels insects from sitting on the plants.

In a study Neoliya *et al.* (2005), found that medium to low doses of Azadirachtin ($P< 0.01$) significantly influenced the total head protein profile in the larvae of *Helicoverpa armiger* (Hubner/Lepidoptera: Noctuidae). Azadirachtin was found effective in reducing the protein concentration at 0.1 μg by tropical application in the 2nd stadium. However, treated larvae did not show the same protein concentration up to 72 hours compared to control. Azadirachtin is one of the most antifeedents against the African desert locust *Schistocerca gregaria*. (The limiting concentration to cause 100% impregnated on to filter paper/nanogram/cm^2). It is very active against African armyworm, some species of chewing insects that occurs in United State (e.g. Japanese beetle) and several scale insects.

Azadirachtin is a potent phagorepellant and shows toxic effects at 0.1 to 1000 ppm when incorporated in to diets of different insect species. Brown rice hopper avoided feeding on plants sprayed with neem oil. *Neem* oil is mostly used for soap manufacturing industry.

PYRETHRUM

It is found in the floral part of Chrysanthemum genus belonging to the family 'compositae' or 'sun flower' family. Only few species of this large family like *Chrysanthemum (Pyrethrum) roseum*. Web and Mohr., *C. cinerariefolium* Trev., *C. marshalli* Ach. and *C. tambutne* have been found to be valuable source of this insecticide. It is known for 100 of years for its insecticidal properties. Aphids and red spiders have been controlled by the application of sprays containing 0.4% pyrethrins. Though pyrethrum was formerly used as finely grounded flowers, today it was used as dust or sprays. Pyrethrum contents of flower head increases up to the time of full opening of the flowers. Pyrethrum flowers are being dried at same temperature (as in sun earlier) viz. 54.4° C. Then the dried flowers are compressed and exported. These flowers are ground to a fine powder and extracted with the solvents. (Misra and Mani, 1994). Pyrethrins are active as Pyrethrins I and II but they are unstable compound as they decomposes when exposed to air or sunrays (Singh *et al.*, 1993) Pyrethrins are toxic contact and stomach poisons. They are non-toxic to human beings. There action is similar to that of DDT. Pyrethrins are used as insect powder (obtained from flower head), oil extracts and water soluble extracts. The Pyrethrins are toxic to insects, which come in contact causing rapid paralysis owing to their effects on the nervous system.

It is relatively harmless to mammals, although it is poisonous if injected in to the blood stream and dust may cause allergic reaction in some people.

ROTENONE

A crystalline substance was isolated by Nayai, 1902; from *Derris cheninsis*. As this plant was known locally as Rohten, the crystalline substances were called Rotenone (Misra and Mani, 1994). Mueholic extract of roots of the fish-poison climber (*Millettia pachycarpa*) controls aphids. This plant contains two insecticidal compounds, Rotenone and Saponin.

Rotenone is a complex isofleovoroid placed in the group. 'Rotenoids' obtained from the roots of plant of genera Darnis, Lonchocarpus and Tephrosia (Singh *et al.*, 1993).

Rotenone acts as stomach poison used in pest control. Extract of Derris roots mixed with pyrethrum are also used as insecticidal sprays. Rotenone is not harmful to man; important sources are *Derriselliptica, D. malaccensis, Lonchocarpus nicon* and *L. utilis*, obtained chiefly in roots but may occur in other parts of the plants like leaves, stem or seeds. Derris and ryania preparations are harmless to men and domestic animals but derris is extremely poison to fish and must not be allowed to contaminate ponds or streams.

NICOTINE

Nicotine, an alkaloid obtained from tobacco (*Nicotiana tobaccum*) is graded as contact insecticides. Nicotine occurs in at least two solanaceous genera, Nicotiana and Duboisia. It is found however, in species completely unrelated to Nocotiana as well *Asclepia syriaca. Atropa belladonna, Equisetum arvense* and *Lycopodium clavatum* (Schmeltz, 1971). Anabasin is obtained from the tobacco (*Nicotiana glauca*) plant. Crude extract of its leaves can be used to control aphids (Singh *et al.*, 1993).

The control of nicotine in leaves of tobacco varies from 0.5% in bland varieties to as high as 15% in some Algerian samples, the average ranging between 2.0 and 30.0% (Misra and Mani, 1994). It has used successfully in the control of aphids, capsids, apple succers, psyllids, midges, grape worms, mealy bugs etc. Nicotine was first of all used as a decoction in 1960, against the bugs in France. In 1773 tobacco smoke was directed on to plants for control of aphids etc. In 1828, its chemical nature was discovered as nicotine sulphate. It is a compound obtained commercially by the action of nicotine with sulphuric acid and used as a contact spray.

Nicotine is highly volatile. Its conversion in to the sulphate lowers its volatility. Nicotine sulphate sprays effectively control many kind of insects and pests (Singh *et al.*, 1993). Though nicotine is usually used as a contact insecticide and when applied in the form of a dust or spray, it probably acts as a fumigants (Misra and Mani, 1994). Nicotine fumes, obtained by evaporation of liquid nicotine base over a heater or by burning nicotine, are important in house fumigation (Singh *et al.*, 1993). As a toxicant to insects, nicotine penetrates directly through the intugement and spiracles. Nicotine acts directly on ganglia of insects CNS producing excitation at lower concentration and paralysis at high concentration. There are several other solanaceous plants (potato family) that contain promising insecticidal properties.

Other commonly known plants pesticides are *Ocimum sanctum, Nyctanthes arbor-trites, Ricinus communis* (castor), *Carum curvi* (Caraway), *Coriandum sativum* (Coriander), *Pinpinella anisum* (Anise), they have effective insecticidal properties.

An experiment was conducted by Bhatia and Kaur (1997) had use three biopesticidal plants (*Azadirachta indica, Ocimum sanctum, Nyctanthes arbor-trites*).

Each of the extract was inoculated in swiss albino mice and its effect on the humoral and cell mediated immuno response was studied. It was observed that the pesticidal plant extracts may prove to be immuno ecofriendly pesticides and an alternate/ antagonistic agents to the non-ecofriendly chemical pesticides.

Insecticides of plant origin would always superior over the other because they are safe and least hazardous to human beings, easily available to use and does not affect the environment and ecology.

REFERENCES

Ambica, S.R. and Jayachandra (1980). *Current Science* 49: 874-875.

Barnyby, M.A. and Klocke, J.A. (1990). *J.Insect. Physiol.* 36: 125-131.

Bhatia, A. and Kaur, J.(1997) In: Evaluation and Immunomodulatory Property of Leaf Extracts of Biopesticidal Plants:An Approach Towards Development of Ecofriendly Pesticide: Proceedings of the International Conference on Industrial Pollution and Control Technologies.17th-19th Nov., Hyderabad. pp. 268-277.

Chandrashekar, K., Kumari, A.,Kalia, V., Gujar, G.T. (2005). Baseline Susceptibility of the American Bollworm, *Helicoverpa Armigera* (Hubner) to *Bacillus Thuringiensis* Berl var karstaki and its Endotoxins in India. *Current Science* 88 (1): 167.

Cronin, D., Moenne, L.Y., Fenton, A., Dunne, C., Dowling, D.N. and O'Gare, F. (1997). Role of 2, 4. Diacetyl Phloroglucinol in the Interactions of the Biocontrol Pseudomonad Strain F 113 with the Potato Cyst Nematode *Globodera Rostochiensis. Appli. and Environ. Microbiol.* 63: 1357-1361.

De Magad, R.A., Bravo, A., Berry,C., Crickmore, N. and Schnept (2003). Structure, Diversity and Evolution of Protein Toxins from Spore forming *Entomopathogenic Bacteria. Annu. Rev. Genet.* 37: 409-433.

Jayaraj, S. (1994): *Biofertilizer and Biopesticide Technology and Sustainable Agriculture and Rural Employment. Ecotechnology and Rural Employment: A Dialogue,* Mc-Millan Press Madras. pp. 230-246.

Kranthi, K.R., Dhawad, C.S., Naidu, S., Mate, K., Patil, E and Kranthi, S. (2005a). *Bt* cotton Seed as a Source of *Bacillus Thuringiensis* Insecticidal

Cry 1 Ac toxin for Bioassays to Detect and Monitor Bollworm Resistance to Bt. Cotton. *Current Science,* 88 (5).

Kranthi, K.R., Naidu, S., Dhawad, C.S., Tatwawadi, A., Mate, K., Patil, E., Bharose, A.A., Behera, C.T., Wadaskar, R.M. and Kranthi, S. (2005b). Temporal and Intraplant Variability of Cry 1 Ac Expressionin *Bt.* Cotton and its Influence on the Survival of the Cotton Bollworm, *Helicoverpa Armigera* (Hubner/Noctuidae: Lepidoptera). *Current Science.* 89 (2): 291.

Lecadet, M.M., Frachon, E., Dumanoir,V.C., Ripouteau,H.,Hamon,S., Laurent,P. and Thiery,I.J. (1999). Updating the H-antigen Classification of *Bacillus Thuringiensis. J.Appl. Microbiol,* 86: 660-672.

Misra, S.G. and Mani, D. (1994): In: *Agricultural Pollution.* Vol. II, Ashish Publishing House, New Delhi.

Neoliya, N.K., Singh, D., Sangawan, R.S. (2005). Azadirachtin Influences Total Nead Protein Content of *Helicoverpa armigera* Hub, larvae. *Current Science.* 88 (12).

Pranshanthi, S.K. and Kulkarni, S. (2005). *Aureobasidium Pullalans,* A Potential Mycoherbicides for Biocontrol of Eupatorium *Echromolaena odorata* (L) King and Robinson J. Weed. *Current Science.* 88 (1): 18.

Rembold, H., Sharma, G.K., Czopplt, C.H. and Schmutterer,H. (1982). *J. Angew Entomol.* 93: 12-17.

Schmeltz, I. (1971): Nicotine and Other Tobacco Alkaloids, In Naturally Occurring Insecticides, M. Jacobson and D.G. Crosby (Eds.), Marcel Dekkar, Inc., New York, 1-585, pp. 91-131.

Schnept, H.E., Lee, S., Dojillo, Jo.A., Burmeister, Paulo., Fencil, K., Morera, L., Nygaard, L., Narva, K.E. and Walt, J.D. (2005). Characterization of Cry 34/35 Binary Insecticidal Proteins from Diverse *Bacillus Thuringienses* Strain Collections. *Applied and Environ. Microbiol.* 71(4): 1765-1774.

Siddique, I.A. and and Shaukat, S.S. (2003a). Suppression of Root Knot Disease by *Pseudomonas Fluorescense* CHAO in Tomato: 2,4-N-acetyl Phloroglucinol. *Soil Biology and Biochemistry.* 35: 1615-1623.

Siddique, I.A. and and Shaukat, S.S. (2003b). Plant Species Host Age and Host Genotype Effects on *Meloidogyne Incognita* Biocontrol by *Pseudomonas Flurescence* Strain CHAO and its Genetically Modified Derivatives. *Journal of Phytopathology.* 151: 231-238.

Singh, O., Nag, P., Kumar, V.K. and Singh, J. (1993). In: Frontiers in Environmental Geography, Concept Publishing Company. New Delhi.

Xiong, L., Li, J. and Kong, F. (2004). *Streptomyces Species* 173 on Insecticidal Micro-organism from Marine Letters. *Applied Microbiology.* 38: 32-37.

Yojana, Controlling Pests: The Natural Way., April. 30, 1992.

8

Sustainable Farming Systems for Today and Tomorrow

H.K. Patro[1], L.R. Patro[2] and S.C. Swain[3]

INTRODUCTION

Population of India in end of 1990 was 840 millions. The estimated population by year 2010 will exceed 1.1 billion, by year 2030, 1.37 billion and by year 2050 it may reach 1.66 billion. We must also remember that bulk of the population in India is between 15 to 45 age group and this can have serious implications on population growth in the next 10 to 20 years unless comprehensive population control measures are adopted (Pandey, 1994).

1. Krishi Vigyan Kendra (Gajapati), Rudragiri - 761016. *E-mail:* pranati_hkp@hotmail.com.

2. Environmental Toxicology Lab. Department of Zoology & Bio-technology, KBDAV College, Nirakarpur, 752019, Orissa, India. *E-mail:* dr.lrpatro@rediffmail.com, dr.lingarajpatro@sify.com

3. Krishi Vigyan Kendra Rayagada, Gunupur, Orissa, India.

FOOD SCENARIO

Increased population will put tremendous pressure on food demand. Food supply in 1987-88 was 189 kg and in 1989-80 it was 210 kg per person per year (i.e. 575 g/day/person). Based on food supply of 1989-90, India will have to produce 245 million tonnes food in year 2010), 289 million tonnes in 2030 and 349 million tonnes in year 2050. If food supply is enhanced by 10 per cent to eradicate mal-nutrition in lower strata of society, the demand will grow to 269 million tonnes in 2010, 318 million tonnes in 2030 and 384 million tonne in 2050.

PERFORMANCE OF FOOD SECTOR

Globally, the share of arable land account for 11%, whereas in case of India, it is 51.5%. But Indian agricultural growth rate compares unfavourably with the growth rate of neighbouring countries. During the past two decades, the growth rate has been 2.8% as against 4.8% in Myanmar, 4.94% in China and 4.92% in Pakistan (Mohapatra, 1994) The food production projection, based on gross cropped area, gross irrigated area, fertilizer consumption, high yielding variety seed use, farm productivity levels, agricultural credit, fertilizer price and output price, is estimate to be 211 million tonnes in 2000, 316 million tonnes in 2030 and 387 million tonnes in 2050 (Table 8.3). The share of rice and wheat will be I largest followed by coarse grain and pulses.

Food demand-supply gap is likely to widen if population continues to grow at faster rate. In-future, the increase in food production in irrigated and favorable rainfed area may be slower if crop technologics are not properly upgraded. The rate of increase in unfavourable conditions will, continue to remain slower in future as well. These two factors may result in widening the demand-supply gap in coming years. Further, the progress at higher level of productivity always remains slower as it can be seen from the Chinese experience of 1981-88.

MATCHING FOOD PRODUCTION WITH POPULATION GROWTH

Land-use Pattern

India had 305 m ha reporting area in 1951. Out of which 119 m ha was agricultural land. 75 m ha was under forest, 25 m ha waste barren land and 67 m ha pasture and fallow (Table 8.1). The land-user under non-agriculture is likely to be 30 m ha in 2000 and will increase to 40 m ha in 2050. This is primarily due to increased demand by growing population. Although per capital land for life support system has decreased from 514 M^2 to 300 M^2 per person and will reduce further to 250 M^2 by 2050. By 2050 increased population will result net agricultural land of 800 M^2 per person for crop production.

Table 8.1: Land-use pattern in India (million ha)

	1951	*1981*	*2000*	*2030*	*2050*
Geographical area	328	328	328	328	328
Reporting area	305	305	318	318	318
Gross usable area	304	304	304	304	304
Forest	75	67	70	73	75
Waste land Barren (Uncultivated)	25	29	30	24	24
Pasture/Fallow	67	45	24	16	10
Life support system (non-Agrl. Land)	18	22	30	36	40
Agril. Land	119	141	150	155	155
Gross area	0.76	0.33	0.30	0.22	0.20
Net Ag. Area	0.30	0.21	0.13	0.12	0.08
Life support system m^2/person	514	319	300	262	250

The total cropped area under rice and wheat in 19.87-88 was 42 m ha and 22:6 million ha will increase substantially by 2050 to meet the growing need of rising population. Similarly total cropped area under pulses, oil seed .and cash crop will increase. increase in total cropped area will be mainly through multiple cropping and increased cropping intensity (Table 8.2).

Table 8.2: The cropped area (in ha) under different crops in 1955-56, 1987-88, 2000 and the projected cropped area in 2050

	Cropped area (in million tones)			
	1955-56	*1987-88*	*2000*	*2050*
Rice	31.5	42.0	44.4	57.2
Wheat	12.4	22.6	31.0	52.0
Coarse grain	32.5	29.8	28.4	23.3
Pulses	23.2	21.6	24.2	30.5
Oil crop	12.1	20.0	22.1	32.0
Cash crop	10.5	10.2	11.9	15.0
Other crops	13.0	33.0	38.0	45.0
Total Cropped Area	135	177	200	255

Table 8.3: The production (m.t.) of various crops from 1955-56 1987-88, 2000 and the projected changes in year 2050

	Production (in million tones)			
	1955-56	*1987-88*	*2000*	*2050*
Rice	27.6	61.3	85.8	161.2
Wheat	8.8	49.7	76.9	158.0
Coarse grain	19.4	20.7	35.5	45.0
Maize	2.6	5.6	10.7	16.4
Jowar	6.7	11.8	18.5	28.2
Bajra	3.4	3.3	6.3	7.4
Pulses	11.0	11.1	12.8	32.8
Total	66.8	138.4	211.0	387.0

Soil Resource

Soil is a most important resource for food production. Out of 304 m ha land area, India has 144.4 m ha area affected by wind and water erosion. Alkali and Saline soil including coastal area is estimated to be 9.1 m ha while water logged area occupies 8.8 m ha. Land covered ravines estimated to be 3.9 m ha. The area under ravine and torrents and shifting cultivation are 2.73 and 4.91 in ha respectively. Thus, total problem area is estimated to be 173.6 m ha.

The total flood prone is estimated to be 40 m ha while total drought prone is estimated to be 260 m ha. The maximum area affected by flood in worst year is reported to be 18.6 m ha but annual average area affected by flood is estimated to be 8.0 m ha. Appropriate corrective measures and conservation can bring a sizable area under cultivation.

Thus out of the geographical area of 328.7 m. ha 79.2 m ha is black soil of various categories and 57.8 m ha is alluviul soil. The soil type-red sandy, red and yellow and grey brown covers 91.4 m ha. Red loamy and laterite total 34.7 m ha. These soils are fairly productive provided good soil management practices including balance nutrient application is adopted. The problem, acid soils require judicious lime application as correction. similarly alkaline soil requires gypsum. amendment for amelioration of the alkali condition.

Water Resource

The ultimate gross irrigation potential! of the country according to revised estimates is 155 m ha. Out of this, 58.5 m ha can be covered by major and medium irrigation, 15 m ha by minor irrigation, surface water and 80 m ha by underground water. After independence, India had a gross irrigated area of 22.6 m ha in 1951. After Five-year Plan, country could develop an irrigation potential of 79.4 m ha. The rate of growth of irrigation development from 1951-52 to 1989-90 was 1.45 m ha per year. All the irrigation potential created through various schemes are not effectively utilized because of management, deficiencies and a lag in the development of the command area. The efficiency of canal irrigation is well below 40% primarily due to seepage loss for main canal and distributaries and field channels further the productivity of canal irrigated area ranges from 1.7-2 t ha^{-1} compared to potential of 7 to 9 t ha^{-1}. The cropping intensity has also not increased sub-stantially. However, the productivity of land irrigated by ground water is 2.5 to 3 t ha^{-1}. and groundwater offers great potential for expansion.

Conjunctive water use (combined use of surface and ground water sources) offers great potential for improving irrigation efficiency. The scope for development of ground water potential is larger in Assam (97%). Orissa (95%), M. P. (90%), West Bengal and Kerala (88%), Karnataka (77%) and Bihar (76%). However, the rate of development of water resources in future will be slow either due to more difficult areas, or land when resource utilization is expensive. The estimated rate of irrigation development in next 60 years will be approximately 1.25 m ha per year as compared to 1.45 m ha per year over past 40 years from 1951 to 1990. Improved irrigation water management will play greater role in improving productivity in future. Drainage in many areas will require special attention as well.

Fertilizer Consumption

India ranks fourth in the world in nutrient consumption. In 1989-90, 11.6 m t of primary nutrients (N+P+K) was consumed as against 145.6 million tonnes of global consumption. India also ranks fourth in the world with 9 million tonnes of ($N+P_2O_5$) production as against global production 126.7 million tonnes. The country does not produce any potash but consumes more than a million tonne per year. The country has attained a sufficiently large production capacity over the period of the past 25 years since the advent of the new fertilizer policy in 1965.

Growth consumption had increased from 0.194 million tonne in 1960-61 to 2.26 million tonnes in 1970-71. During seventies the growth had accelerated from 2.26 million tonnes to 5.5 million tonnes in 1980-81. During eighties growth rate has been uneven and the consumption has reached to 11.6 million tonnes in 1989-90.

In AD 2010 demand consumption may grow to 17.50 million tonnes. Out of 27.5 million tonnes the share of N P_2O_5 and K_2O will be 16.5, 6.3 and 2.7 million tonnes respectively. The gap between demand and supply will increase progressively to over three million tonnes for nitrogen and 0.36 million tones for P_2O_5. Our estimate for nutrient consumption matches with these estimates reported here. Further our estimate for 2050 is 35 million tonnes for N + P+K to produce 387 million tonnes of foodgrain for a population of 1.66 billion. The basic question is, can we meet all the demand through chemical fertilizer If not what are other avenues to supplement. Our estimates indicate that 20-25 per cent of N+P+K can be mobilized through organic sources such as FYM, crop residue city waste, green mature, bio-fertilizers, and other waste.

The realization of 25% (N+P+K) by 2010, through organic sources can be made if 200 million tonnes of FYM, 30 million tonnes of crop residue returned to soil, 25 m ha of green manure cultivation and 10 million tonnes of urban and rural wastes. By 2050 the substitution of 25% (N+P+K) will require 400 million tonnes FYM, 100 million tonnes crop residue, 50 m ha of green manure and 50 million tonnes of urban and rural waste.

Improved Seed Supply

Seed as an input in modern crop production plays an important role in increasing the farm productivity. Seed is a product of crop improvement programme which is combined effort of a multidisciplinary team-breeders pathologists, entomologists, agronomists and physiologist. An improved cultivar is visually more productive an efficient input user and tolerant to biotic and abiotic factors. Development of need based cultivars with superior triats will remain a continuous activity of agricultural development. Therefore, Supply of such input to 100 m farmers will also require continuous efforts to develop infrastructure needs.

Seed industry in India has developed over past 30 years. The annual rate of HYV seed use by farmers has been 1.81 m ha yr^{-1} from 1965 to 1987. With this rate6f HYV seed use, the country will require infrastructural development of seed supply for 200 m ha by year 2050.

SOIL AND CROP MANAGEMENT TECHNOLOGY

Improved soil and crop management contributes 25% towards from productivity. These practices include better tillage and land preparation, timely crop establishment and optimum plant density, proper crop nutrition and water management and adequate crop protection measure. Importance of improved crop management technology in rainfed are as becomes more evident.

In future, if we have to match food production with increasing population, our farmer must upgrade their crop management practices through adoption of improved technology. Our crop husbandry practices at Farm level are often below the expectation for high farm productivity.

FACTORS AFFECTING FOOD PRODUCTION

Food production is result of additive effects of all production factors in proper combination. To increase the food production at a rapid rate to match the rapidly growing population, we must expand the key components of production are process. The components of Production are gross area, gross Irrigation, fertilizer consumption, improved seed use soil and crop management, agricultural credit. procurement price, fertilizer price, fertilizer use level and social environment.

The first nine factors directly contribute towards farm output. The social and political environment which also includes peace and tranquility, is also important for rapid agricultural development.

CAN INDIA SUSTAIN ITS FOODGARIN PRODUCTION BY 2050

Future rate of food grain production in next 40 years will depend on three factors.

1. Efficient resource management;
2 Bridging the gap between current farm yield and potential farm yield of conventional technology; and
3. Improving the yield potential of current germplasm through conventional and biotechnological tools.

Soil and water resource management must continue to find high priority and resource basic must continuously be expanded by scientific management practices. The low farm productivity must be upgraded to the potential level through adoption of improved crop management technology. In this regards. On Farm Research must find high priority in research planning in next century to realize full farm yield potential.

FARMING SYSTEM APPROACH TO MAXIMIZE FARM PRODUCTIVITY

Integration of farm enterprisers:

1. Cropping;
2. Livestock;
3. Aquacuhure;
4. Agro-Horticulture or Agro-forestry offer opportunity to farmers to raise their farm income.

A farmer may have one, two, three or all four enterprises his farm at his farm. However their integration into a viable farming system depends on bio-physical resources, technical soundness, socio economic environment and management skill of the farmers.

Cropping

Crop production constitutes a sizable portion of farm income followed by live stock and Agro-horticulture system or aquaculture.

Development of efficient, need based cropping system to match the growing needs of farmers' family and community will continue to find high priority in agricultural research. To support cropping system research. the component technology improved cultivar, right kind of farm machinery, pesticides and better soil and water management practices must be developed to match the systems requirement. Such glaring example is, rice-wheat-legume system in Northern India. where rice cultivars must be water regime specific - upland lowland (irrigated, shallow rainfed and deep water) and wheat cultivar must fit in different date of planting when soil moiqure becomes favourable for wheat planting after harvest of rice. A short duration legume such as mungbean urd-bean or cowpea can he planted with minimum till-age and irrigation to maximize the economic return. Similar examples exist in rice-rice-legume system in South India, Bajra-wheat and Groundnut-wheat system in Western state', a suitable mix of grain and fodder crop is essential for mixed farming system.

Livestock Integration

Crop-livestock integration is a old age practice of Indian farmers. In present context, crop-livestock integration must consider continuing need of growing family size of small farmers. Small farm of 0.5 to 1 ha must adopt a cropping system that support a reasonable number of animals that generate enough drought power and income to small farmers.

Intergrated farming system involving crops and animals must consider an appropriate combination of animals (cow, buffalow, pig, goat, sheep and poultry) and crops that maximizes the return per unit of investment to small farmers. This should also optimize the farm family labour and skill.

Integrated farming system involving livestock must also harmonize the land use for other economic activities of small farmers for sustainable development.

Aquaculture

Incentive to integrate aquaculture farming system generates additional income and improve the nutrition of small farms. Aquaculture includes fish, shrimp, lobsters, salmons, moluses and crustaceans. The important fish are tuna, tilapia and carp. Although, interest in the farming of shrimp and prawns continue to increase but the fish farming offers the greatest potential.

Nation policies and local management are important to control access to capital and ensure adequate returns on investment on aquaculture. In coastal areas, small farmers can integrate rice and aquaculture and increase their income. In land quaculture, farming includes community tank, pond, water ways and rivers. In-land aquaculture must harmonize the land-use for other economic activities fro sustainable development.

Agro-forestry and Fruit crops

A well-managed agro-forestry and orchard can continue to provide massive amount of energy, food as well as jobs and income. They are strong potential base for generating economic growth and social development. More effective strategies and commitment are therefore, needed for conservation, re-agro-forestation and management of orchard as well as for ensuring the appropriate integration of agro-forestry and orchard into land use and rural programmes. Agro-forestry and orchard management must be harmonized with other land use to ensure sustainable development.

PROCESSING OF SURPLUS PRODUCT AND RECYCLING OF RURAL SOURCES OF RAW MATERIALS

Increased employment and income from farm can come from establishment of rural industries. These industries must utilize surplus product and recycle the rural bye product and waste. For example more than on third of paper needed in the country can be manufactured from straw bamboo and begasse. This emphasizes utilization of non-wood fibres, both economically and ecologically because it helps to conserve health material and financial resource but it require special efforts in design, financing, planning, supplying marketing and the procurement of raw materials. Another examples of processing of perishable Farm product like potato and tomato. Development o small scale industry necessitates mill design which ensure adequate supply of raw material over several months and sale point of the product. Such investment generates more employment and income of farm labour and alleviate the poverty and social environment.

APPROACH TO FUTURE AGRICULTURAL DEVELOPMENT

Sustainable development in agricultural context, should not allow natural resource (soil and water) degradation, but promote economically and ecologically sound soil and crop management practices through adopting a integrated farming system which must consider six parameters:

1. Production efficiency;
2. Economic incentive;
3. Energy use;
4. Employment generation;
5. Environmentally friendly technology; and
6. Equity.

With increasing population and limited land, the key to sustainable development will be our ability to develop and introduce ecologically sound technologies to raise the potential productivity on marginal land and reverse its current wide spread degradation as well as to raise significantly the productivity of high potential in order to take the pressure of marginal land. High potential land can be enhanced to generate greater yields without damaging its future yield capacity. High yield potential areas are either irrigated or reliable and adequate rainfall during the crop growing season and soils are productive.

Low potential land in general can not be exploited intensively for stable food crops and will be used under utmost care without degradation. Low yield potential areas are either unreliable rainfall or poor productive soil.

The strategic approach that can be adopted in developing sustainable faring system in four regions of the country is listed below.

North India

High yield irrigated areas of Punjab, Haryana, and Uttar Pradesh are major one.

Food security and the alleviation of rural poverty will continue to depend on establishing sustainable production in the high potential areas. Not only it is essential to maintain and increase staple food production on irrigated land to feed the rural an d urban poor but it is also essential that natural resource management be improved.

High potential areas can generally sustain intensive crop production using existing technologies as long as care is taken not to exceed the soil's generative capacity, soil fertility is generally high or has the potential to be so. Current agricultural technology is capable of raising the "Population carrying capacity" of such lands. Unfortunately poor water management has led to water logging and salinity in some areas. In other cases, indiscriminate use of fertilizers and pesticides is a problem.

Sustainability issue must be addressed in high productive irrigated areas through;

- Integrated farming system
- Improved soil and water management
- Integrated post management
- Integrated crop management practices that are environmentally friendly and cost effective.
- Balanced utilization of under ground water resource.

East India

East India includes primarily Bihar, Orissa, West Bengal and Assam, East India has both "high risk period "July-Oct" and risk free-high production potential period "Nov-June."

In high risk period, flood and drought are major sources of problem which makes difficult to develop appropriate technology, moderate increase is only possible in future in high risk period. However, in risk free-high production period the great potential exists for raising crop production. Exploitation of under ground water can bring prosperity in the region by increasing food productiol8 three to four folds. Unfortunately in past all efforts has been in short term perspective. Government policies lacked long term planning. The maximization of farm productivity in eastern India must centre under two management strategies, "High risk and risk free period."

During this period section of crop and cultivars to match the landuse system used on water regimes and management practices that increase input use efficiency in high risk (flood/ drought) period. Rice productivity can be enhanced in shallow rainfed, and deep water by dry seeding of single or an inter-crop of early and late maturing rices to reduce risk of crop failure and increase the land productivity. During drought period, rice must be irrigated by deep well either by exploiting underground water resource and/or stored rain water.

In upland system, upland rice management system must be altered and managed like a "wheat crop" and irrigate the rice crop when needed where irrigation facilities exists. In areas where irrigation facilities cannot be developed, upland rice can be inter-cropped with upland crop or replaced by upland crop completely.

The ultimate answer to bring prosperity in this region is development of underground water resource. The administrative reform and political commitment of necessary resource and land tenure system can bring quick result. Technological changes have demonstrated that it is possible to raise two crops during this period with productivity of 6 to 8 t ha^{-1}. For example cultivation of wheat of 3-4 t ha^{-1} is possible followed by summer pulses of 1-1.5 t/ha. Rabi Maize of a yield potential of 6-7 t is possible to grow in many areas. Potato, oil seed and pulses can also be grown. In some areas rice is second profitable alternative. The vegetable cultivation can enhance income of farmers around cities. To achieve a successful food production programme a network of deep well either operated by electricity or petroleum fuel must be set up by farmers themselves or by Government subsidy.

We must learn how to utilize the farm resources including underground water to increase the income of the poor farmers.

West India

In the low-potential areas, arid and semi arid tropic zone of Gujarat, Rajasthan, Maharashtra and Karnataka and Madhya Pradesh, the existing conditions don't favour accelerated agricultural development. The upper limit for crop production is restricted by limited rainfall and irrigation potential. Due to abnormal distribution of rainfall, productivity of land in rainfed agriculture is low. Run off, erosion and the drainage pose serious problems for most semi-arid areas of this country. The conservation and collection of excess water and its utilization on watershed management to provide stability in crop production. In arid parts of the country, there is not much opportunity for harvesting and storing rain water. The adoption of efficient tools for moisture conservation, weed control and by increasing the water "holding capacity of soil with the use of local organic matter resources may upgrade the production.

Integrated farming system involving agro-forestry and animal offers better prospect of developing sustainable land-use system to support rural population. In these areas, pearl-millet, sorghum, barley, groundnut, cowpea and other minor legumes are main crops. Practices of alley cropping and shelter belt of leguminous shrub for feed resource and use of fruit and trees with appropriate cropping system must be promoted.

South India

In South India, sustainable development in irrigated area must include integrated farming system, improved water management and integrated nutrient and pest management must find high priority. Increased input use efficiency and improved soil and water management to accelerate the productivity level with adoption of integrated crop management practices to reduce cost of production must be targeted. The cropping intensity should be increased from two to three crops per year. Production of integrated farming system involving animal, poultry and aquaculture will increase income of small farmers. In rainfed areas, an approach to efficient watershed management be promoted to maximize the land-use system involving appropriate cropping system, agro-forestry fruit crops and livestocks. Proper mix enterprisers at farm will enhance the income of resources resource poor farmers. Use of leguminous shrub/trees should be planted in cropping/strip cropping system to recycle the nutrients and conserve soil and water resources.

POLICY PLANNING IN SUSTAINABLE FARMING SYSTEM DEVELOPMENT

Sustainable development is a pattern of social and structural economic transformation which optimizes the economic and other social benefits available to the present without jeopardizing the likely potential. As a result agricultural policymakers must choose between efficiency and equity with the goal of national food security. There is also need to consider income and employment for alleviation the hunger and poverty. Balanced emphasis on rainfed will help the poorest regions and on irrigated will strengthen the overall food security.

FUTURE RESEARCHABLE AREAS TO DEVELOP SUSTAINABLE FARMING SYSTEM

Following areas of research that need attention to sustain needs of present and future generation, are listed below:

1. Ecosystem based land-use system that combines water and crop management practices should be developed. Community level resource management strategies for short and long-term basis should be evolved.

2. Empahsis needs to be placed on multi-disciplinary analysis that link policy and market issue, farmer decision-making and the interaction among the crops, livestock trees and soil components of farming systems. Emphasis needs to be placed on farming systems. Emphasis needs to be placed on understanding specific farm structure and function

characteristics that directly affect farm system sustainability. Methodologies and analytical tools are needed to understand farmer decision-making and to analyze the interactions among crops, livestock trees and soils.

3. Ecosystem based cropping system that combines mixed farming and agro-forestry system, should have high research priorities. Geramplasm enhancement of existing and new crops, to develop improved cropping systems must be accelerated. Sustainability could be improved by better residue and stubble management. Research is needed to develop inter-crop and sequential multiple cropping systems that combine cereals and legumes to enhance crop productivity while maintaining soil productivity.

4. Emphasis should be placed on nutrient inputs from plant residues, green manure crops, animal manures, fertilizers and other implement to increase the crop performance and soil productivity. Nutrient cycling system need to be analyzed in various agro-ecological zones in order to develop integrated nutrient management systems.

5. Integrated farming system should consider improved interaction of crop, livestock, aquaculture and fruit trees shrubs including leguminous and baceous plants that could improve nutrient cycling and enhance both environmental quality and farmer income. In intensively cultivated areas, research is needed to improve dairy and meat production systems by developing diverse feed resources.

6. The understanding of farmer traditional wisdom and analysis of past and present farm systems under normal stress and exceptional stress, essential on farmer level decision making process and community level resource management.

The use of archaeological methods and history of past civilizations could contribute to the understanding of general principles of sustainability.

REFERENCES

ICAR. 1998. *National Agricultural Technology Project. Main Document*. Indian Council of Agriculture Research, New Delhi.

Mohapatra, I.C. 1994. Farming Systems Research: A Key to Sustainable Agriculture. *Fertilizer News* 39 (11): 13-25.

Pandey, R. K. 1994 *Sustainable Farming Systems Developments for Food Needs of Present and Future Generation*.

Randhawa, M.S. 1980. *A History of Agriculture in India*. ICAR, New Delhi, Vol. pp. 105-129.

9

Managing Climate Change in 21st Century
A Challenge to Global Community

Prof. B.P. Mahapatra[1]
Dr. S.K. Chaudhary[2]

ABSTRACT

Globalization phenomenon along with recognition of Earth as a global common necessitates a global action to solve multi-lateral issues in trade, finance, environment spread of infectious diseases and security. Millennium Development Goals (MDG) determined in the global summit in 2000 bears the testimony. In that summit eight different well-defined goals were set. The goal number 7 of the MDG is to ensure the environmental sustain-ability. This article is going to throw light on a major challenge to global community that is climate change. Its impact, its adaptation and mitigation, environmental governance will also be discussed in the article.

1. Faculty member in Alphia Institute of Business Management, Berhampur, Orissa. *E-mail:* bhabaniprasadmahapatra@gmail.com

2. Faculty member in Alphia Institute of Business management, Bhubaneswar, Orissa. *E-mail:* sumankalyan72@gmail.com

INTRODUCTION

Sustainable development has been defined as "development that meets the needs of the present without compromising the ability of future generations to meet their own needs." However, the global warming and climate change have severely affected the prospects of sustainable development. Climate change refers to a statistically significant variation in either the mean state of the climate or in its variability, persisting for an extended period (typically decades or longer). Climate change may be due to natural internal processes or external forcing, or to persistent anthropogenic changes in the composition of the atmosphere or in land-use.

The Earth is the only planet in our solar system that supports life and which has an atmosphere of the proper depth and chemical composition. The atmosphere carries out the critical function of maintaining life-sustaining conditions on Earth, in the following way: each day, energy from the sun (largely in the visible part of the spectrum, but also some in the ultraviolet, and infra red portions) is absorbed by the land, seas, mountains, etc. If all this energy were to be absorbed completely, the earth would gradually become hotter and hotter. But actually, the earth both absorbs and, simultaneously releases it in the form of infra red waves. All this rising heat is not lost to space, but is partly absorbed by some gases present in very small (or trace) quantities in the atmosphere, called GHGs (greenhouse gases). Greenhouse gases (for example, carbon dioxide, methane, nitrous oxide, water vapour, ozone), re-emit some of this heat to the earth's surface. If they did not perform this useful function, most of the heat energy would escape, leaving the earth cold (about - 18° C) and unfit to support life. However, with the advent of Industrial Revolution 150 year ago, man-made activities have added significant quantities of GHGs to the atmosphere. The atmospheric concentrations of carbon dioxide, methane, and nitrous oxide have grown by about 31%, 151% and 17%, respectively, between 1750 and 2000. An increase in the levels of GHGs could lead to greater warming, which, in turn, could have an impact on the world's climate, leading to the phenomenon known as climate change. So effects of climate change.

Some effects of climate change are given below:

1. The polar and inland regions are affected more swiftly than the oceans and tropics.Increasing temperature is likely to lead to increasing precipitation.

2. The IPCC Third Annual Report says: "global average water vapor concentration and precipitation are projected to increase during the 21st century".

3. The *American Insurance Journal* predicted that "catastrophe losses should be expected to double roughly every 10 years because of increases in construction costs, increases in the number of structures and changes in their characteristics." The Association of British Insurers has stated that "limiting carbon emissions would avoid 80% of the projected additional annual cost of tropical cyclones by the 2080s. The cost is also increasing partly because of building in exposed areas such as coasts and floodplains".

4. A study (published in *Science*) of changes to eastern Siberia's permafrost suggests that it is gradually disappearing in the southern regions, leading to the loss of nearly 11% of Siberia's nearly 11,000 lakes since 1971. At the same time, western Siberia is at the initial stage where melting permafrost is creating new lakes, which will eventually start disappearing as in the east.

5. According to a UN Climate report, the Himalayan glaciers that are the sources of Asia's biggest rivers—Ganges, Indus, Brahmaputra, Yangtze, Mekong, and Yellow—could disappear by 2035 as temperatures rise. Approximately 2.4 billion people live in the drainage basin of the Himalayan rivers. India, China, Pakistan, Bangladesh, Nepal and Myanmar could experience floods followed by droughts in coming decades. In India alone, the Ganges provides water for drinking and farming for more than 500 million people.

6. Increased levels of CO_2 have led to ocean acidification. Furthermore, as the temperature of the oceans increases, they become less able to absorb excess CO_2. Rising sea levels are due to thermal expansion and melting of glaciers and ice sheets, and warming of the ocean surface, leading to increased temperature stratification. Other possible effects include large-scale changes in ocean circulation. The amount of oxygen dissolved in the oceans may decline, with adverse consequences for ocean life.
7. From 1961 to 2003, the global ocean temperature has risen by 0.10° C from the surface to a depth of 700 m. There is variability both year-to-year and over longer time scales, with global ocean heat content observations showing high rates of warming for 1991 to 2003, but some cooling from 2003 to 2007.
8. The IPCC Fourth Assessment Report predicts that many mid-latitude regions, such as Mediterranean Europe, will experience decreased rainfall and an increased risk of drought, which in turn would allow forest fires to occur on larger scale, and more regularly. This releases more stored carbon into the atmosphere than the carbon cycle can naturally reabsorb, as well as reducing the overall forest area on the planet, creating a positive feedback loop.
9. Climate change is projected to affect the development process. According to Nicholas Stem, former chief economist of World Bank in 2006 recommended one per cent of global Gross Domestic Product (GDP) should be invested to mitigate the effects of climate change, and that failure to do so could risk a recession of twenty percent of global GDP. Roads, airport runways, railway lines and pipelines, (including oil pipelines) may require increased maintenance and renewal as they become subject to greater temperature variation. Initially it was thought that global warming was affecting agricultural yields because of role of carbon dioxide in photosynthesis especially preventing photorespiration which is responsible for significant

destruction of several crops. In Iceland, rising temperatures have made possible the widespread sowing of barley, which was untenable 20 years ago. Whilst there is evidence to suggest some areas like the US and Siberia will benefit significantly from global warming, other evidence suggests that global yields will be negatively affected. For example Africa is likely to worst affected because of its vulnerability geographically and 70 per cent of its population rely on rain-fed agriculture for their livelihoods. Tanzania's official report on climate change suggests that the areas that usually get two rainfalls in the year will probably get more, and those that get only one rainy season will get far less. The net result is expected to be that 33% less maize—the country's staple crop—will be grown. In 2007, higher incentives for farmers to grow non-food bio fuel crops combined with other factors (such as rising transportation costs, climate change, growing consumer demand in China and India, and population growth to cause food shortages in Asia, the middle east, Africa, and Mexico, as well as rising food prices around the globe. Many of the world's largest and most prosperous cities are on the coast, and the cost of building better costal defenses (due to the rising sea level) is likely to be considerable. Some countries will be more affected than others—low-lying countries such as Bangladesh and the Netherlands would be worst hit by any sea level rise, in terms of floods or the cost of preventing them. In developing countries, the poorest often live on flood plains, because it is the only available space, or fertile agricultural land. These settlements often lack infrastructure such as dykes and early warning systems. Poorer communities also tend to lack the insurance, savings or access to credit needed to recover from disasters. The combined effects of global warming may have particularly harsh effects on people and countries without the resources to mitigate those effects. This may slow economic development and poverty reduction and make it harder to achieve the Millennium Development Goals.

10. Some Pacific Ocean island nations, such as Tuvalu, are concerned about the possibility of an eventual evacuation, as flood defence may become economically unviable for them. Tuvalu already has an *ad hoc* agreement with New Zealand to allow phased relocation. In the 1990s a variety of estimates placed the number of environmental refugees at around 25 million. The IPCC estimated that 150 million environmental refugees will exist in the year 2050, due mainly to the effects of coastal flooding, shoreline erosion and agricultural disruption.

11. Increasing global temperature means that ecosystems will change; some species are being forced out of their habitats possibly to extinction because of changing conditions, while others are flourishing. Secondary effects of global warming, such as lessened snow cover, rising sea levels, and weather changes, may influence not only human activities but also the ecosystem. Rising temperatures are beginning to have a noticeable impact on birds, and butterflies have shifted their ranges northward by 200 km in Europe and North America. Plants lag behind, and larger animals' migration is slowed down by cities and roads. In Britain, spring butterflies are appearing an average of 6 days earlier than two decades ago.

12. The immediate ecological and economic impact, the huge dead forests provide a fire risk. Even many healthy forests appear to face an increased risk of forest fires. because of warming climates. Pine forests in British Columbia have been devastated by a pine bettle infestation, The infestation, which (by November 2008) has killed about half of the province's lodgepole pines (33 million acres or135,000 km^2) is an order of magnitude larger than any previously recorded outbreak and passed via unusually strong winds in 2007 over the continental divide to Alberta. Besides forest fires in Indonesia have dramatically increased since 1997 as well. These fires are often actively started to clear forest for agriculture. They can set fire to the large peat bogs

in the region and the CO_2 released by these peat bog fires has been estimated, in an average year, to be 15% of the quantity of CO_2 produced by fossil fuel combustion.

13. Mountains cover approximately 25 per cent of earth's surface and provide a home to more than one-tenth of global human population. Changes in global climate pose a number of potential risks to mountain habitats and human uses.

14. Sea level rise is projected to increase salt-water intrusion into groundwater in some regions, affecting drinking water and agriculture in coastal zones. Increased evaporation will reduce the effectiveness of reservoirs. Increased extreme weather means more water falls on hardened ground unable to absorb it, leading to flash floods instead of a replenishment of soil moisture or groundwater levels. In some areas, shrinking glaciers threaten the water supply. The continued retreat of glaciers will have a number of different effects. In areas that are heavily dependent on water runoff from glaciers that melt during the warmer summer months, a continuation of the current retreat will eventually deplete the glacial ice and substantially reduce or eliminate runoff. A reduction in runoff will affect the ability to irrigate crops and will reduce summer stream flows necessary to keep dams and reservoirs replenished.

15. The most direct effect of climate change on humans might be the impacts of hotter temperatures themselves. People with heart problems are vulnerable because one's cardiovascular system must work harder to keep the body cool during hot weather, heat exhaustion, and some respiratory problems increase. Higher air temperature also increases the concentration of ozone at ground level. In the lower atmosphere, ozone is a harmful pollutant. It damages lung tissues and causes problems for people with asthma and other lung diseases. Due to global warming, infectious diseases such as dengue fever, malaria may increase. The WHO says global warming could lead to a major increase

in insect-borne diseases in Britain and Europe. The WHO estimates 150,000 deaths annually "as a result of climate change", of which half in the Asia Pacific region.

INTERNATIONAL AGREEMENTS

The issue of climate change has been included on the political agenda of the world community as far back as the middle of the1980s. In 1988, the World Meteorological Organization (WMO) and the United Nations Environment Programme (UNEP) established the IPCC—a forum for thousands of scientists. The same year, for the first time, the United Nations General Assembly (UNGA) took up the issue of climate change. A resolution was adopted for the "Protection of Global Climate for Present and Future Generations of Mankind." In 1990, the IPCC released its First Assessment Report in which it confirmed the threat of climate change and recommended a special global agreement. The scientists' call was backed up by another resolution by UNGA that served as the basis for creation of the UN Framework Convention on Climate Change (UNFCCC), which entered into force in 1994. At present, more than 190 countries are parties to the convention; only a few small developing countries have not joined it yet.The Kyoto Protocol, unanimously adopted at the Third Conference of Parties (COP3) to the UNFCCC in Kyoto in December 1997 has become the most important step in international efforts to prevent climate change. The protocol established the targets for greenhouse gas emissions for industrialized countries from 2008 to 2012. The entry of the protocol into force required ratification by at least 55 countries, representing a minimum 55% of 1990 greenhouse gas emissions, which happened on 16 February 2005, after Russia ratified the Kyoto protocol at the end of 2004.The three pillars of the Kyoto Protocol are its flexibility mechanisms: the Clean Development Mechanism (CDM), Joint Implementation (JI) and Emissions Trading.

Clean Development Mechanism are projects to reduce greenhouse gas emissions measured in Certified Emissions

Reductions (CER) units, which can be transferred to the project investor. There are about 2000 projects. The projects involve about 50 countries. China leads in the total volume of CDM projects, followed by India, Brazil and other countries. In general, by 2012 the Kyoto Protocol will likely have managed to generate more than 3000 CDM projects with total volume of emissions reduction of approximately four billion tonnes of CO_2, and the minimum amount of climate investments will reach US$ 30 billion. This inflow of CER units will make it possible for industrialized countries to satisfy their demand for acquisition of emission quotas for meeting their Kyoto commitments.

Joint Implementation includes projects in Annex I countries that are financed by other (Annex I) countries. These reduce greenhouse gas emissions (in 2008-2012 time frame), measured in Emission Reduction Units (ERUs), which in accordance with article 6 of the Kyoto Protocol can be transferred to the project investor or acquirer of ERUs representing an Annex I country.

Emission trading is under the Article 17 of the Kyoto Protocol which introduces the sale and purchase of greenhouse gas emission permits with Assigned Amount Units (AAUs) between Annex B countries. Emissions trading between all Annex B countries started in 2008. Currently the trade is carried out in individual countries or groups of countries in accordance with their internal agreements. Even though the Kyoto Protocol is being criticized for its ecological weakness but we should not forget that this agreement is the first specific action based on quantitative commitments rather than merely declarative statements. This protocol has given astrong foundation of new agreement. And the negotiations of this new agreement were launched some time ago and are well under way. The new protocol is to be approved at COP15 Copenhagen in December 2009. A number of meetings can be referred to as milestones on the road to Copenhagen, namely COPs in Bali in December 2007, Bonn in June 2008 and Accra14 in August 2008. COP14 was held in Poznan, Poland, in December 2008, along with a meeting of the parties to the Kyoto Protocol.

Today, there are numerous suggestions by various countries regarding important provisions for the Copenhagen agreement: adaptation of developing countries to the effects of climate change and their financing, the application of a sectoral approach to specific emissions reduction in energy-intensive economic sectors, the problem of tropical deforestation, etc. Many experts believe that quantitative emission reduction targets and mandatory U.S. participation will substantially strengthen the agreement. Some countries have already announced their intentions. The 27-member European Union is ready to reduce emissions by 20% of 1990 levels by 2020. If other countries undertake similar commitments, the reduction level might reach 30%. Japan is ready to reduce emissions by 14% of its 2005 level by 2020. Both the EU and Japan intend to achieve partial reduction by purchasing quotas through the CDM or other mechanisms. Even before the 2008 Accra meeting, South Africa announced that it intended to stabilize its currently growing rate of emissions by 2025 and then begin efforts to reduce them. At Accra, South Korea formally declared that it would announce its emissions reduction and limitation targets in2009. A number of other countries, notably Armenia, expressed readiness to undertake commitments subject to relevant assistance provided by industrialized countries. In 2004, Russia took a significant step in combating climate change when it ratified the Kyoto Protocol. Indeed, at that time the protocol's destiny depended on Russia, since the United States - the major source of greenhouse gases emissions - refused to ratify it. Now the time has come for a new international agreement and new actions aimed at mitigating climate change.

ENVIRONMENTAL GOVERNANCE IS THE KEY

Multi-level inter-actions (i.e., local, national, international/ global) among, but not limited to, three main actors, i.e., State, market, and civil society, which interact with one another, whether in formal and informal ways; in formulating and implementing policies in response to environment-related demands and inputs from the society; bound by rules, procedures, processes, and widely-accepted behaviour; possessing characteristics of "good governance"for the purpose of attaining environmentally-sustainable development. There are three major hurdles for an effective environmental governance. They are jurisdictional gap, information gap, and implementation gap.

JURISDICTIONAL GAP

The discrepancy between a globalized world and a set of inescapable transboundary problems on the one hand, and a dominant structure of national policy-making units on the other, has led to a gap in issue coverage. The UN Charter provides for no environmental body. Responsibilities are instead divided among agencies, including the Food and Agriculture Organization, the World Meteorological Organization, the International Maritime Organization, the International Oceanographic Commission, the UN Educational, Scientific and Cultural Organization, the Commission on Sustainable Development, the Global Environment Facility, and the UN Development Programme, with a coordinating and catalytic role assigned to the UN Environment Programme (UNEP). Besides that there are independent secretariats to the numerous treaties, all contending for limited governmental time, attention, and resources. The Economic and Social Council of the UN has the gigantic task of coordinating all of these diffused efforts. The scattering of environmental activities across many international organizations has greatly compromised participation, especially that of developing countries. Negotiations on critical pollution control and natural resource management issues often occur simultaneously around the world. Also the costs associated with attending intergovernmental sessions to negotiate international environmental agreements and treaties are high, both in terms of direct economic expenses and opportunity costs. Countries with limited diplomatic and financial resources have thus been forced to choose which conferences to attend, or whether to attend them at all. Again most environmental agreements have no procedures for resolving disputes among parties. For example, Other treaties, like UN Framework Convention on Climate Change, expressly defer disputes to the International Court of Justice (ICJ). And while the ICJ has set up an "environmental chamber", it has never heard a case. As a result of the weakness of the environmental institutions, the disputes they might have addressed end up being taken to other fora, such as the World Trade Organization.

INFORMATION GAP

Sound decision-making depends on the availability of information regarding environmental problems, trends, and causal relationships, and policy options, results, and compliance with commitments. Data collection, "indicator" development, monitoring and verification, and scientific assessment and analysis thus emerge as central to sound decision-making. High quality data with cross-country comparability is necessary to support an effective approach to problem definition and assessment. However, significant data gaps remain. Compliance monitoring and reporting are even more unsystematic, scattered, and informal.

IMPLEMENTATION GAP

The biggest single obstacle to environmental progress at the global scale is the lack of an action. This might be attributable to an implementation gap. Treaty congestion has led to overload at the national level, where the political, administrative, and economic capacity to implement agreements resides. Even industrialized states with well-developed regulatory mechanisms and bureaucracies have become overwhelmed.The existing financial mechanisms are scattered across the Global Environment Facility, UNEP, the World Bank, and separate treaty based funds such as the Montreal Protocol Finance Mechanism. This dispersion and lack of integration reinforces the perception of a lack of seriousness in the North about the plight of the South. A multi-pronged strategy should be adopted to address these gaps in global environmental governance.

CONCLUSION

There has been no change in the position of the Government of India on the principles agreed to under the UNFCCC since 1992. Industrialised countries are responsible for about 83 per cent of the rise in cumulative fossil-fuel-related carbon dioxide emissions since 1800. Even in 2004, industrialized countries, which account for only a fifth of the global population, contributed nearly half of the annual greenhouse gas emissions. The contribution of India to global carbon dioxide emissions is around four per cent, but it is growing fast owing to a high economic growth rate. It is not clear whether India has any alternative proposals if the global negotiations to raise the targets for reduction of emissions for industrialized countries, which are scheduled to conclude by 2010, fail. Failure to come to any new agreement for enhanced reduction commitments or even an emission reduction commitment at the rates agreed under the Kyoto Protocol is bad news for all.

REFERENCES

Energy Bulletin Quarterly Edition January-February 2009.

Ravindranath, N.H., *Storm Warning by Frontline*, February 24 March, 2009, 2007.

Revitalising Global Environmental Governance: A Function-driven Approach. Daniel, C. Esty and Maria H. Ivanova.

Various *IPCC Assessment Reports*.

Various Annual Reports of UNEP.

Various Reports COP Conferences.

Website of Ministry of Environment and Forests, Government of India.

10

Some Changes in Haemolymph Biochemical Composition with Sex and Size of the Freshwater Crab, *Sartoriana spinigera* (Wood Mason, 1871)

P. Nayan[1], R. Pandey[1]
R.N. Prasad[1], S. Besra[1] and U.P. Sharma[1]

ABSTRACT

The freshwater crabs (Decapoda-Crustacea) *Sartoriana spinigera*. He profusely found in large numbers in shoreline areas of the ponds, lakes, wetlands and paddy fields of Jharkhand. These crabs are rich source of protein and their raw meat contains about 20% protein, 1.2% minerals and little fat and hardly any carbohydrate. It is a fact that crabs provide an important means of livelihood for the local tribal people.

Very little is known about the basic biolosry of this organism. Basic information of its life cycle and physiological

1. Zoology Department, Ranchi College, Ranchi University, Ranchi - 834 008, Jharkhand (India).
Email: nayan_pankaj@yahoo.com

parameters are completely lacking. To evaluate the health and physiology of this wild population of crab, biochemical parameters of its haemolymph were determined from collection of adult (male and female) and juvenile (male and female) crabs. Crab's haemolymph parametel's fluctuate according to their external environment, developmental stage and reproductive cycle. Variation in the biochemical composition of total proteins and albumin has been studied. It has been observed that all these parameters are functions of sex and size. There is negative correlation between mass of crab and the protein in the haemolymph of both sexes in adult crab, but in juvenile crab the protein content is significantly higher.

In male crab plasma albumin concentration was 1.25 ± 0.30 g/dl and in female it was 1.54 ± 0.39 g/dl.

INTRODUCTION

- Proteins are the most abundant compounds in serum, because they are the basic component of enzymes, many hormones, antibodies and clotting agents. It plays a major role in maintaining the delicate acid base balance.
- The serum proteins serve as a reserve source of energy for the tissue and the muscle, but environmental as well as sexual changes often disturb concentration of haemolymph protein and also disturb the acid base balance.
- A considerable amount of informations are available for many Decapoda, particularly European species (1960).
- The haemolymph protein concentration in *Callinectes sapidus* and accumulated two facts: (i) individual variation of haemolymph protein concentration showing ten-fold range; and (ii) male crabs showed a distinctly lower mean value than females for protein concentration.
- The total protein represents the sum of albumin and globulin and hence it is also important to know which protein fraction is high or low. Albumin is very strong

predictor of health. Albumin's presence in the plasma creates an osmotic force that maintains fluid volume within the vascular space.

- In the present investigation also along with total protein concentration albumin concentration has also been estimated.

MATERIAL AND METHODS

- The freshwater crabs *Sartoriana spinigera* were collected from the local market and brought to the laboratory of Ranchi College, Ranchi and was kept in large sized aquarium having little water and sand.
- After acclimation adult and juvenile males and females were separated by observing the abdomen and considering the body weight. Crabs having body weight less then 20 g were selected as juvenile and more than that were selected for adult group.
- Before taking haemolymph samples experimental crabs were weighed. Haemolymph sample were taken withdrawing 0.5 to 1 ml haemolymph from each crab using hypodermic needle, inserted through the arthrodial membrane at the base of chelate or 4th or 5th walking legs. These samples were used for the determination of total protein and albumin.
- Total protein was determined by Biuret method with the help of commercially available kit (Erba Mannhein) using bovine serum albumin as a standard. The intensity of blue color developed was proportional to the concentration of plasma protein which was read at 546 nm in semi-autoanalyser (Erba Mannheim - CHEM 5 Plus V_2)'.
- Albumin was estimated by B.C.G. Dye method with the help of commercially available kit (Erba Mannhein). The blue green colour formed was proportional to the concentration of albumin present. It was read at 630 nm in semi-autoanalyser (Erba Mannheim - CHEM 5 Plus V_2).

RESULTS

Total plasma protein concentration in different weight groups of adult males (18.68-90.56 g) and adult females (24 - 57.3 g) were shown in Table 10.1 and Table 10.2 respectively. Average total plasma protein concentration in adult male was 5.52 ± 1.76 gldl, whereas average total plasma protein concentration in female was only 3.71 ± 1.22 g/dl.

Table 10.1: Estimated value of total plasma protein concentration (g/dl) in different weight groups (g) of adult male crabs, *S. spinigera*

Sl.No.	*Body weight of adult male crabs (g)*	*Total plasma protein conc.(g/dl)*
1.	90.56	8.39
2.	88.2	7.12
3.	85.49	7.05
4.	82.78	6.93
5.	80.07	6.85
6.	77.36	6.8
7.	71.94	6.65
8.	66.52	6.49
9.	58.72	6.16
10.	49.3	5.46
11.	38.56	5
12.	31.68	4.6
13.	27.72	3.96
14.	24.08	3.78
15.	21.3	2.68
16.	20.44	2.55
17.	18.68	3.24
Average		5.512353
S.D		± 1.76469
r		0.968587

Table 10.2: Estimated value for total plasma protein concentration (g/dl) in different weight groups of adult female crabs, *S. spinigera*

Sl. No.	*Body weight of adult female Crab (g)*	*Total plasma protein conc. (g/dl)*
1.	57.3	3.27
2.	57.16	3.74
3.	50.68	2.86
4.	44.44	4.63
5.	42.22	2.86
6.	41.1	5.24
7.	39.62	3.67
8.	39.04	3.51
9.	36.66	3.2
10.	35	3.98
11.	34.92	4.68
12.	33.26	3.01
13.	24	3.96
Av.		3.739231
SD		± 0.746307
r		-0.19296

These means were analyzed statistically using Student's t-test and these showed that the difference between these two means were highly significant ($p < 0.001$).

When the data for plasma protein concentration in adult male crabs were plotted against body weight, they depicted a straight line with a slope value ($b = 0.062$) and intercept ($a = 2.060$). The plasma protein concentration showed a positive correlation with body weight ($r = 0.969$; $P < 0.001$) (Fig. 10.1).

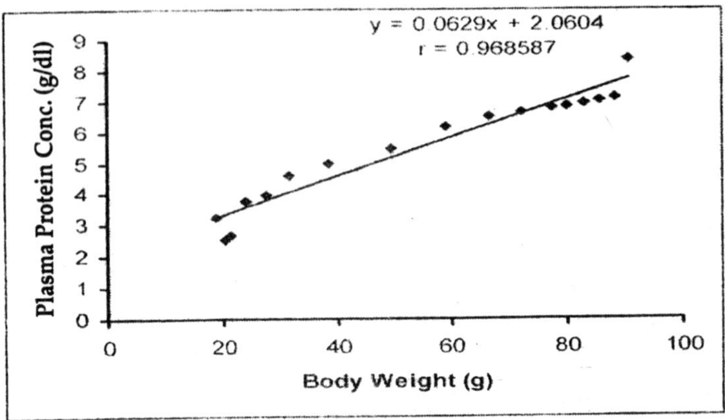

Fig. 10.1: Graph between Body weight (g) of adult male Vs plasma protein concentration (g/dl) in *S. spinigera*

Fig. 10.2 showed graph plotted between body weight and protein concentration in adult female crabs, which showed slight negative correlation (r = -0.192).

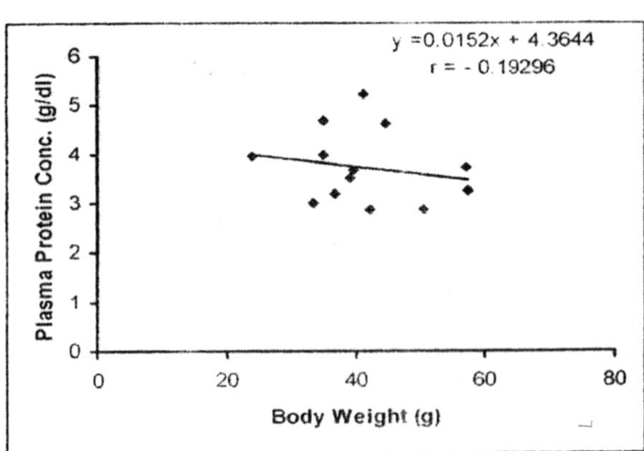

Fig. 10.2: Graph between Body weight of adult female (g) Vs plasma protein concentration (g/dl) in *S.spinigera*

Tables 10.3 and 10.4 showed the concentration of plasma protein in immature (juvenile) male and immature female crabs respectively in different weight groups. In juvenile female

(7.28-15.94 g) the average plasma protein concentration was 3.40 ± 1.16 gldl and in juvenile male (9.9-13.44 g) average plasma protein concentration was 5.25 g/dl. Statistical analysis of these two means was done using t-test and difference between these means was not found significant.

Table 10.3: Estimated value of total plasma protein concentration (g/dl) in different weight groups of juvenile male crabs, *S. spinigera*

Sl. No.	*Body weight of juvenile male crab (g)*	*Total plasma protein conc. (g/dl)*
1.	14.23	3.82
2.	13.44	4.05
3.	12.68	4.21
4.	11.92	4.36
5.	11.45	4.49
6.	11.22	4.56
7.	10.98	4.62
8.	10.68	4.65
9.	10.64	5.29
10.	10.3	7
11.	9.9	8.51
Av		5.050909
S.D		± 1.4291
r		-0.71802

Table 10.4: Estimated value for total plasma protein concentration (g/dl) in different Body weight groups (g) of juvenile female in *S. spinigera*

Sl. No.	*Body weight of juvenile crab(g)*	*Total plasma protein conc.(g/dl)*
1.	15.94	3.83
2.	14.9	3.63
3.	13.98	3.42
4.	13.32	3.95
5.	12.4	3.9
6.	11.5	3.85
7.	10.32	2.18
8.	9.56	2.44
9.	8.8	2.7
10.	7.28	3.22
Av		3.312
SD		±0.653891
r		0.630072

Figure 10.4 showed the graph plotted between body weight of juvenile female and plasma protein concentration, which gave a significant positive correlation (r = 0.630) where as Figure 10.3 showed an negative correlation (r = -0.718) between these variables in juvenile male.

Table 10.5 Average male albumin concentration observed was (1.25 ± 0.30 g/dl) (Table 10.5). Statistical analysis revealed that correlation between body weight and plasma albumin concentration was positively significant (r = 0.9244). Figure 10.5 the graph plotted between these parameter shows that effect of size is expressed as a power function of body weight. Concentration of albumin increased with a slope value (b = 0.0124) and intercept (a = 0.754).

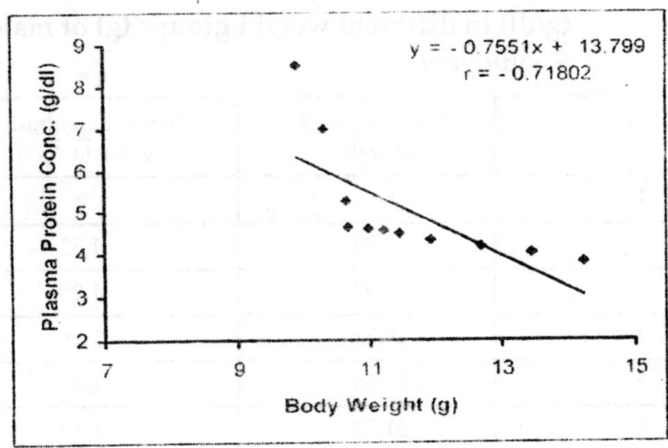

Fig. 10.3: Graph between Body weight of juvenile male (g) vs plasma protein concentration (g/dl) in *S. spinigera*

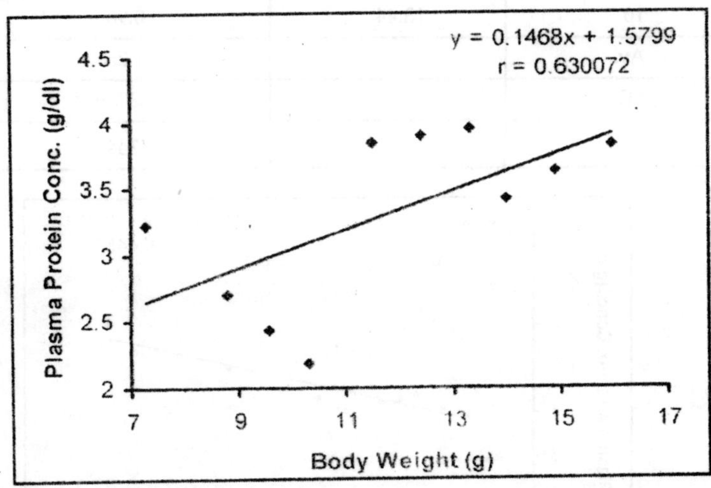

Fig. 10.4: Graph plotted between Body weight of Juvenile Female (g) Vs plasma protein concentration (g/dl) in *S. spinigera*

Table 10.5: Estimated value of plasma Albumin concentration (g/dl) in different weight groups (g) of male crabs *S. spinigera*

Sl. No.	*Body weight of male crab (g)*	*Plasma concentration of albumin (g/dl)*
1.	88.2	2
2.	63.38	1.52
3.	50.97	1.28
4.	44.77	1.16
5.	38.56	1.05
6.	31.32	1.12
7.	27.7	1.15
8.	24.08	1.19
9.	18.76	1.07
10.	13.44	0.96
Av.		1.25
SD		± 0.303937
r		0.924455

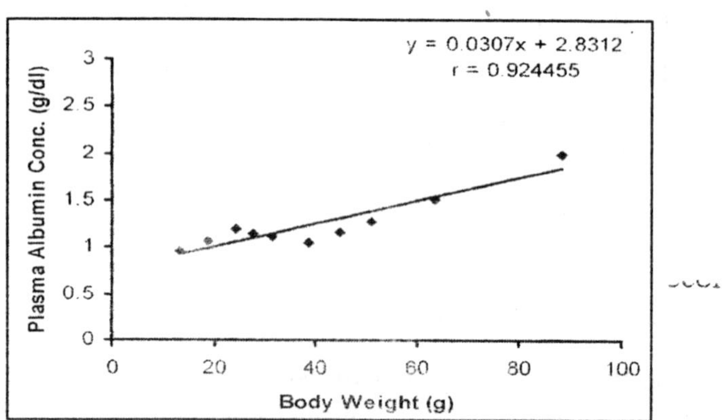

Fig. 10.5: Positive correlation between body weight (g) and plasma concentration (g/dl) of albumin in male crabs, *S. spinigera*

The estimated value of plasma albumin concentration in different weight groups of female crab is shown in Table 10.6. Average female albumin concentration was 1.55 ± 0.399 g/dl. The graph plotted between body weight (g) and plasma albumin concentration of female crab with a slope value (b = - 0.030) and intercept (a = 2.831). They express negative correlation (r = - 0.615) (Fig. 10.6).

Table 10.6: Estimated value of plasma Albumin concentration (g/dl) in different weight groups (g) of female crabs *S. spinigera*

Sl. No.	*Body weight of female crab (g)*	*Plasma albumin conc. (g/dl)*
1.	57.3	1.26
2.	42.22	1.28
3.	40.63	1.32
4.	39.04	1.36
5.	36.98	1.8
6.	34.92	2.25
Av.		1.545
SD		± 0.399587
r		-0.61532

DISCUSSION

Present investigation showed that freshwater crab's haemolymph protein concentration is a function of sex and size, physiological condition as well as reproductive cycle of the crab. Both adult and juvenile male contain significantly higher concentration of the total plasma protein (5.52 g/dl and 5.24 ± 1.65 g/dl) respectively than adult female (3.6 g/dl ± 1.22 and 3.31 ± 1.16 g/dl) respectively, which signified more growth in males than females.

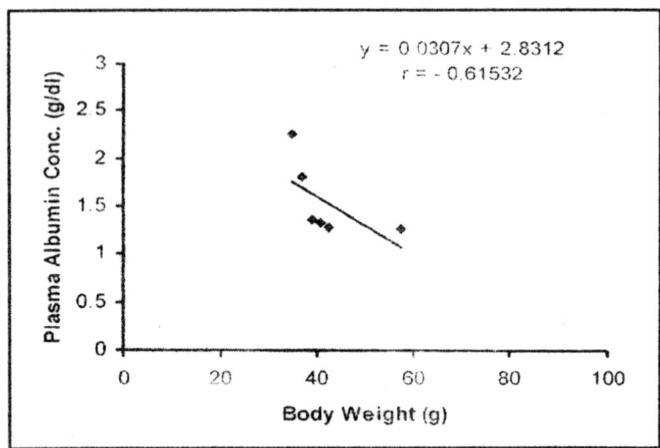

Fig. 10.6: The Positive correlation between body weight (g) and plasma concentration (g/dl) of albumin in female crabs, *S. spinigera*

There is a positive correlation between the mass of crab and the concentration of plasma protein.

In case of juvenile males, where plasma protein concentration is negatively correlated (r = - 0.690) with body mass i.e. lower the body weight and higher the plasma protein concentration. It signified that in young male crab had higher metabolic rate as well as higher growth rate.

Stephen *et al.,* (2002) studied the horse shoe crab, *Limulus polyphemus* haemolymph biochemical parameters and reported that the biochemical values fluctuate their osmolality and other haemolymph parameters according to their external environment, developmental stage and reproductive cycle. According to them total plasma protein concentration in *Limulus polyphemus* was 8.15 g/dl. This value is slightly higher in the present crab i.e. 5.51 g/dl.

The difference observed in the adult female plasma concentration was due to the difference in their reproductive stage because samples were collected from the female in the month of July and August 2007, when the most of the females were in post-oviposition stage i.e. ovary were in resting or spent phase.

Another important observation was that in adult females the correlation between body weight and plasma protein concentration was slightly negative (r = - 0.1917), this fluctuation was only due to the presence of different concentration of female specific protein (FSP) during the different stages of oocyte development.

It is reported that FSP in the haemolymph were always higher prior to the maximum accumulation of yolk in the oocytes, but they dropped off markedly prior to oviposition.

11

Ecosystem Management
Issues and Trends

Dr. S.K. Chaudhury[1]
Manaswini Patra[2]
Prof. Ashok Kumar Panda[3]

INTRODUCTION

Over the course of the past century, the understanding of the nature of ecosystems has evolved. In the formative stages of the ecosystem concept, it was common to imagine that ecosystems were relatively simple, closed, fragile, and static. In the past half century research has shown that ecosystems are complex, open, robust, and dynamic. The growing realization that disturbances, both natural and anthropogenic, have played an important role in the establishment and development of

1. Faculty Member, Alphia Institute of Business Management, Bhubaneswar. *E-mail:* sumankalyan72&gmail.com.

2. Librarian, The Techno School, Bhubaneswar, *E-mail:* manaswinibbsr@gmail.com

3. Campus Co-ordinator, Alphia Institute of business Management, Bhubaneswar. *E-mail:* abhinash00@yahoo.co.in

forests has been central to the development of the current understanding of the nature of ecosystems. Improving environmental performance can be just as important externally. Americans expect companies in their communities to operate in an environmentally sound manner. As more information is made available over the Internet, citizens can go online and find out about toxic emissions, compliance with environmental standards, and more. An EMS provides the structure to measure how well your environmental management program is working. By measuring progress against goals, and proactively reporting the results, you can help build public trust and credibility.

Today, many States are establishing special programmes to recognize environmental leadership. Likewise, EPA has a leadership programme of its own. The National Environmental Performance and Track Programme provide top environmental performers with public recognition, information resources, and opportunities for regulatory and administrative flexibility. Having an EMS is a prerequisite for Performance Track membership, if you would like to find out more about the programme please visit the Website at *www.epa.gov/performancetrack*.

What is an Ecosystem?

An ecosystem is a community of biotic and a biotic elements operating as an inter-functional unit. Columbian Basin, The Ganges estuary, wetlands, Savannah, Kalahari desert, rainforest, coniferous forest, etc., are examples of popular ecosystems. Ecosystems may differ in size, range, diversity and relationships. All elements of an ecosystem adjust and modify over time. Certain changes may be the result of natural cycles such as the carbon content or dissolved gas cycles; or due to environment disasters, human movement and settlements, industrialization, war and other interfaces with the environment.

DEFINITION OF ECOSYSTEM MANAGEMENT

Many people and organizations have defined ecosystem management. The following examples represent a cross-section of definitions. There are two themes common to most of these definitions of ecosystem management:

1. management should maintain or improve ecosystems; and
2. ecosystems should provide a range of goods and services to current and future generations.

A great challenge to the implementation of ecosystem management is defining what we mean by "management". As will be discussed in the decision-making process section, management decisions within a hierarchy must be made at each level in the hierarchy. Because of the differences among levels in the hierarchy, the types of decisions that are made at each level will be considerably different. Focusing the ecosystem management debate on the merits and limitations of one particular silvicultural system (e.g., clear cutting) ignores the higher scale management decisions that are equally critical to managing multi-scale hierarchical systems. Therefore, it is important to consider carefully how we conceptualize management and the decision-making process for complex systems. First, we must think about how to manage information at different scales and how to use this information to make decisions at each level in the hierarchy. Once that has been achieved, tools to deliver and process that information can be developed or adapted from existing technology. Only then is it possible to discuss management in terms of operational details (e.g., which trees to plant or cut).

THE TEN DOMINANT THEMES OF ECOSYSTEM MANAGEMENT

Global outlook towards the environment is changing radically. This shift may be largely attributed to demographics. Various natural resource practices are conducted across the world through research and management projects all aimed at an ecologically balanced ecosystem. Certain themes arose from these practices; they do not necessarily represent the value of ecosystem management, but they are a beginning point:

- **Hierarchical Context**: Spotlight on a singular level of the biodiversity hierarchy is inadequate.
- **Ecological Boundaries**: Management necessitates working across administrative and socio-political restrictions and defining ecological boundaries at appropriate scales.
- **Ecological Integrity**: Ecological Integrity is protection of total local diversity and the geographic outlines and developments that maintain that diversity.
- **Data Collection**: Ecosystem management requires more study and data assortment also optimal management and use of existing data.
- **Monitoring**: Mangers must take responsibility of the consequences of their actions so that achievement or fails may be assessed quantitatively.
- **Adaptive Management**: Adaptive Management states that science is temporary and centers on management as a knowledge process or incessant experiment where integrating the consequences of previous feats permits managers to be bendable and adapt to ambiguity.
- **Cooperation:** Ecological boundaries and systems need collaboration between international, national, State and local management agencies along with private bodies.
- **Organizational change**: Implementation of ecosystem management principles needs alteration in the outline of land management bodies and their operation.
- **Humans embedded in nature**: Man is deeply connected to nature. People have elementary controls on the ecological *status-quo* and are in turn impacted by them.
- **Values:** Whatever be the role of scientific comprehension, human values play a leading role in ecosystem management.

SOCIETY FOR PROMOTING PARTICIPATIVE ECOSYSTEM MANAGEMENT

Society for Promoting Participative Ecosystem Management is a non-profit, non-governmental organization working in the area of Natural Resource Management (NRM) primarily in the rural areas. It is committed to the principles of sustainable and rational use of natural resources, equity and social justice in the distribution of benefits especially to the disadvantaged sections such as dalits, landless, women, democratic and decentralized governance of these resources. As an organization committed to these principles, SOPPECOM extends its support to grassroots groups working on NRM issues through training, resource literacy, participatory planning, research and policy advocacy.

Within the broad spectrum of rural livelihood issues, water resource management, along with land, biomass and renewable energy, forms the core of SOPPECOM's concerns. Support for organizing people into legal associations as user groups for participative management of eco-system resources, primarily water has been one of the key activities of SOPPECOM for more than a decade. In its initial phase it piloted various action research programmes around sustainable use of land and water, low external input cropping practices, alternative technology for buildings and water storage structures that have helped develop broad norms for equitable access to resources and their sustainable use. From defining equity within the command areas of irrigation system, SOPPECOM in its subsequent experiments progressed into extending the idea of equity.

ECOSYSTEM CLASSIFICATION

The hierarchical organization for description of the scale of ecosystems is:

1. Domain;
2. Division;
3. Province; and
4. Section.

The classification of ecosystem types is based on examined properties and present knowledge properties like climate, types of vegetation, soil types and water. The global millennium ecosystem assessment, a UN endeavour to assess the health of the earth's ecosystems, has categorized ecosystems under the following:

Marine, Coastal, Inland water, Forest, Dry land, Island, Mountain, Polar, Cultivated, Urban.

Why use ecosystem management?

Human well-being, food security and sustainable livelihoods are intimately linked to the future health of our diverse ecosystems. Ecosystem management demands an *understanding of the functions of ecosystems* in supporting and regulating the processes which underpin life on earth. Furthermore, the approach recognizes that *ecosystems provide diverse goods and services* which are directly or indirectly valued by society in ecological, economic and socio-cultural terms.

Many conventional approaches to resource management have usually been single-purpose and limited in space (e.g. local, regional, national and transboundary) and time (e.g. short-, medium- and long-term). The resulting decision-making processes have therefore generally failed in being able to address the human-induced pressures on the environment in terms of understanding their effects on essential ecosystem services.

Ecosystem management, in recognizing the critical role humans have as managers of biodiversity, aims to avoid these short-comings by identifying and communicating the benefits and values of healthy ecosystems in ensuring both species survival and human well-being.

A PRACTICAL VIEW OF ECOSYSTEM MANAGEMENT

The potential for ecosystem management is being tested and realized in diverse case-studies around the world. In following the five identified IUCN-CEM themes of: Ecosystem

Approach; Ecosystem Restoration; Ecosystem Indicators; Ecosystem Management Tools and Ecosystem Services, this page will provide links to relevant case studies, publications, information and tools that emphasize the practical application of nature valuation for management across a range of ecosystem types. Specifically, there is a focus on how *ecosystem services* can be used as a *basis for valuation* (e.g. ecological, economic and socio-cultural valuation methods). Furthermore, attention will be given to how valuation stimulates the maintenance of ecosystem services through *financing mechanisms, equitable decision-making processes* and *practical objectives* for the management of ecosystem services.

ISSUES

A primary objective of ecosystem management is to maintain the characteristics and processes of the whole ecosystem that sustain component species and human uses, although definitions of ecosystem management differ with regard to the importance placed on sustaining human use. Ecosystem management is usually presented as an alternative to trying to manage for a multitude of species based on their individual habitat requirements. Because any ecosystem can exist in a range of different states and successional conditions, ecosystem management requires some guidance when it comes to determining the desired relative abundance and distribution of ecosystem types and conditions. In the absence of a clear understanding (in this case, of ecosystem dynamics), people are forced to shape decisions based on their beliefs or philosophical outlook. There are at least three general schools of thought with regard to determining desired ecosystem conditions across landscapes, which I refer to as "species-based reserves", "range of natural variation", and "structure-based management".

Under the species-based reserve approach, ecosystem conditions are determined by meeting the population needs of focal species, usually called "indicator" or "keystone" species. This common approach allocates the best remaining habitat to the reserves that are able to support met populations of the species of interest, provides habitat for species dispersal among reserves, and intensively manages the surrounding landscape for other goals. However, despite efforts to maintain genetic diversity, species with low dispersal rates could become genetically isolated in reserves. Other reserve-based approaches argue that areas large enough to encompass natural disturbance and recovery processes (e.g., large fires) and to support all native biota (e.g., wide-ranging carnivores) are required.

LATE-SUCCESSIONAL AND OLD - GROWTH FORESTS

"Late-successional forest" refers to a range of forest conditions that develop over time, beginning with stands in which tree crown expansion slows, openings between trees become larger and more stable, and large, standing dead and fallen trees begin to accumulate (see Fig.11.1, Fig. 11.2, Fig. 10.3 and Fig. 11.4). This includes older ("old-growth") stands in which the oldest trees reach their maximum sizes, understory trees form multiple canopy layers, and dead wood accumulates to high levels (U.S. Forest Service and USDI Bureau of Land Management 1994: B-3).

Definitions of "old-growth", the most widely used definition applies minimum standards related to the density of large trees, diversity of tree species, range of tree sizes, occurrence of multiple canopy layers, and abundance of snags and logs (Old-Growth Definition Task Group 1986). The minimum criteria for Douglas-fir old-growth forests in the western hemlock (*Tsuga heterophylla*) zone are:

Fig. 11.1: A young forest with a relatively simple structure and composition

Fig. 11.2: An old-growth forest with a complex structure and composition

Fig. 11.3: A river with a relatively simple structure, lacking coarse sediment and woody debris

Fig. 11.4: A creek with a complex structure

CONCLUSION

The forest is a bless of God and of a life saving and sustaining one. The complete ecology depends upon the conservation of forest. Unlike a human the forest too have life and the death possibility is high in case in India because of the natural calamities, frequently visible. The growth of a forest depends the conservation of its to the extent that it is less utilized by human. If the ratio is more it likely kills the present growth rate and gradually the diminish happens which disturbs the whole system. Government and its people should strive hard to nurture the forest and uplift its grow and maintenance which is a must. Presently, there are organization those who are keen and initiating to have eco imagination so that they go on creating a base and plan out to implement " NO DESTRUCTION " at all. No doubt we can say to save life one has to save forest first. The old forest has to be replaced but growth is not seen. The soil and water gets disturbed due to the destruction of forest and its population. Foreign aids are in the queue to create and sustain the forestry inventory. This should continue and the public awareness need to be made with due law to punish those who do not save it.

Human well-being and progress towards sustainable development are vitally dependent upon improving the management of earth's ecosystems to ensure their conservation and sustainable use. But while demands for ecosystem services such as food and clean water are growing , human actions are at the same time diminishing the capability of many ecosystems to meet these demands. Ecosystem management ensures that the flow of environmental, economic and social goods and services is maintained. Involvement at various levels is needed, right from stern protection to restricted harvesting.

12

Growth Estimation Through Length-Weight Relationship (LWR) of *Rhabdosargus sarba* and *Jerreomorpha setifer* in Two Ecological Sectors of Chilka Langoon Orissa (India)

Subodha K. Karna,[1] Manas M. Baliarsingh[2] Lingaraj Patro,[3] and Sudarsan Panda[4]

ABSTRACT

The Length-weight relationship (LWR) was studied in *R. sarba* and *J. setifer* collected from two ecological sectors of Chilika lagoon during April 2008 and December 2008. The

1. Chilika Development Authority, C-11, BJB Nagar, Bhubaneswar, Orissa, India. *E-mail:* subodhcda@gmail.com.

2. Department of Zoology and Industrial Fish and Fisheries, Godabarish Mahavidyalaya, Banapur, Orissa, India.

3. Environmental Toxicology Lab. Department of Zoology and Biotechnology, K.B.D.A.V. College, Nirakarpur, Orissa, India. *E-mail:* dr.lrpatro@rediffmail.com.

estimated statistical parameters of the length-weight relationship were presented together with the number of sample measured (N), the size range (min. and max.), mean and standard deviation of the 'b' value (growth rate) calculated in monthly basis in a season and regression coefficient (r^2) derived for males and females separately. The growth rate (b value) of *R. sarba* was estimated as 3.018 for the lagoon in which 3.028 for males and 3.009 for females. In *J. setifer,* the value was 2.9 ranges from 2.892 for males and 2.913 for females. Seasonal variation in pre-monsoon, monsoon and post-monsoon were estimated along with the sectoral variation in both the brackish water and fresh water zone of the lagoon. The values were also estimated in male, female and both the sexes in combine. Estimation of growth rate (b value) in two species of perch through LER were presented for the first time in Chilika lagoon.

Key words: Ecological sectors, Length-weight relationship, Regression co-efficient, Chilika lagoon.

INTRODUCTION

Representatives of different ecological guilds (marine, freshwater and diadromous species) are present in the coastal brackish water zone (Ustups *et al.*, 2003). Bays, estuaries and lagoons are the coastal systems play an important role in the reproduction, growth, and protection of many marine teleosts (Boehlert and Mundy, 1988; Miller and Dunn, 1980; Monteleone, 1992; Yoklavich *et al.*, 1992). This happens only due to an intensive energy exchange occurs between estuaries and coastal waters because of transport of organic matter, nutrients, and organisms. A high diversity of environments that stems from the mixing of marine and freshwater environments provides advantageous habitat conditions for many fish species and results in a high variation of fish assemblages (Repeeka, 2003; Oliva-Paterna *et al.*, 2006). These waters are inhabited by numerous marine fish species since brackish basins provide excellent conditions for the development of fish at their larval and juvenile stages (Lobry *et al.*, 2003; Perez-Ruzafa *et al.*, 2004).

Shallow marine waters are generally considered to be important nursery areas, environments where juvenile fishes will experience enhanced survival and growth (Rozas and Odum, 1998). As the Chilika lagoon is estuarine in nature, assemblages of marine (southern sector), brackish (central sector) and fresh water (northern sector) conditions due to which high biodiversity is observed. The cyclical fluctuation in different hydro-physico-chemical parameters facilitates the biological alteration in the ecosystem.

In fish, LWR has the important role in fishery resource management (Fafioye *et al.*, 2005; Ferhat *et al.*, 2007) and also useful for comparing life history and morphological aspects of populations inhabiting different regions (Gonçalves *et al.*, 1997). These data are needed to estimate growth rates, length and age structures, and other components of fish population dynamics (Kolher *et al.*, 1995). Length-weight relationships allow fisheries scientists to convert growth-in-length equations to growth-in weight in stock assessment models (Gonçalves *et al.*, 1997; Morato *et al.*, 2001; Ozaydin Taskavak, 2007), estimate biomass from length frequency distributions (Petrakis and Stergiou, 1995; Anderson and Gutreuter, 1983), and calculate fish condition (Petrakis and Stergiou, 1995). Length-weight relationship with age data can give information on the stock composition, growth, mortality, maturity, life span assessment (Amin *et al.*, 2008; Bolger and Connoly, 1989).

In case of Chilika lagoon, some studies has been conducted on fish faunal study (Choudhuri, 1916a, b, c, 1917; Bhatta *et al.*, 2001), biodiversity assessment (Mohapatra *et al.*, 2007). But growth assessment and length-weight relationship study is very limited. The present paper documented studies relating to the growth assessment through length-weight relationship of two species namely, *R. sarba* and *J. setifer* which is first attempted so far in Chilika lagoon.

MATERIAL AND METHODS

Study Area

The lagoon is the largest coastal wetland ecosystem in Indian sub-continent. It is an important Ramsar site (No.229) of India. The pear shaped lagoon is situated at 19°28′- 19° 54′ N and 85° 05′- 85° 38′ E. The water-spread area of the lagoon varies between 906 km² to 1165 km² during summer and monsoon months respectively. The total lagoon is divided into four ecological sectors (Fig. 12.1) i.e., Northern sector in fresh water zone, Central is brackish, Southern is marine type but the Outer Channel sector in marine in nature but during monsoon it becomes fresh as 52 rivers and rivulets entering the lagoon in the northern sector discharging their fresh water load through outer channel sector. So the lagoon is mostly estuarine in nature. It is also a great bio-diversity site comprising 267 species of fishes, 28 species of prawn and 35 species of crab were recorded in the lagoon. The fisheries output in Chilika ecosystem shares more than 71% of the economic value of the lagoon.

Sampling

Length-weight relationship study was carried out in 1411 sample of *R. sarba* and 859 sample of *J. setifer*. The specimens were collected from northern and central sector (Figures 12.1) of Chilika lagoon during the seasonal surveys giving importance to the first week of the month between April 2008 and December 2008. For pre-monsoon season, the data were collected in April and May for two months. Similarly, for monsoon and post-monsoon season, the data were collected in July-August and November-December of 2008 respectively. For the above analyses the fish samples were collected randomly inside the lagoon from the fishing boats and also from the landing centre. The *Rhabdosargus sarba* samples were caught by gill nets of mesh size 36-58mm and *Jerreomorpha setifer* samples were collected from the boats fishing with gill nets of mesh size 18-42mm. Both the samples were also collected from Khonda nets (fixed net) of mesh size 8-16 mm. The collected samples were transported to

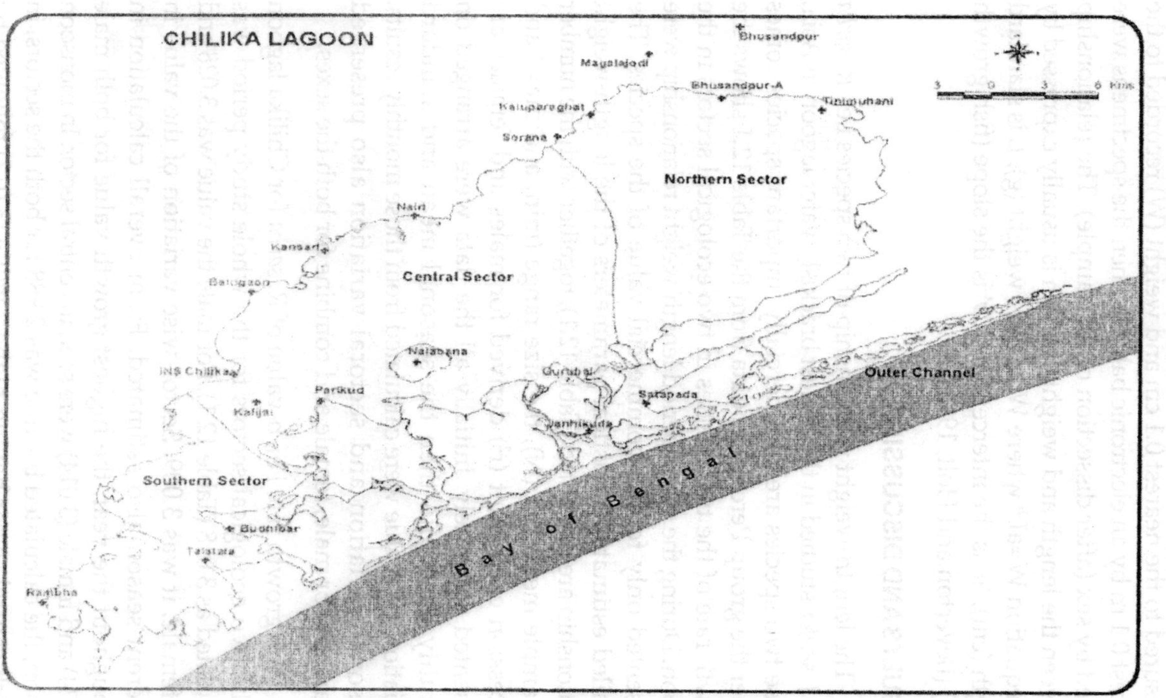

Fig. 12.1: Chilika map showing Northern sector and Central sector

the research laboratory in polythene bags for measurement of length and weight. In the laboratory, Standard length (L) measured to the nearest 0.1 cm and weight (W) recorded to the nearest 0.1 m by an electronic balance, then the specimens were sorted by sex (after dissection of the sample). The relationship between the length and weight of a fish is usually expressed by the equation $W=aL^b$ where W is body weight (g), L is standard length (cm), '*a*' is the intercept and '*b*' is the slope (fish growth rate) (Beverton and Holt, 1996).

RESULTS AND DISCUSSION

The length-weight relationship of two species i.e., *R. sarba* and *J. setifer* studied in the largest brackish water lagoon in Asia. These two species are commercially important species comes under the group Perch. The data from the Table 12.1 shows the growth rate of the two species in two ecological sectors in the lagoon. During the study period length-weight relationship were presented only for the commercial value of the species. The detailed estimated statistical parameters of the length-weight relationship are presented (Table 12.1), together with the number of sample measured (N), the size range (min. and max.) and regression coefficient (r^2) derived for males and females are presented separately. Initially all the data were arranged on monthly basis and then the seasonal mean and standard deviation of b-value were calculated from those monthly results. Seasonal variation and sectoral variation also presented separately for male, female and combine for both the sexes.

The growth rate i.e., b-value of *R. sarba* for Chilika lagoon in the two ecological sectors for the whole study period was calculated as 3.018 (Table 12.1). For male the value was 3.028 and for female, it was 3.009. Sector-wise variation of the value in different season also estimated. From overall calculation in throughout the year, the highest growth value for both male (3.034) and female (3.014) were seen in central sector. In monsoon season, the calculated b value was 2.988 for both the sectors, in which central sector having highest value (3.017) followed by

Table 12.1: Estimated growth rates of *R. sarba* and *J. setifer* during the study period in Chilika lagoon

	Period	*Parameter*	*Central Sector*			*Northern Sector*		
			M	*F*	*Both*	*M*	*F*	*Both*
R. serba	**Pre-Monsoon**	*NS*	87	103	190	112	42	154
		LR (mm)	77-209	89-254	77-254	91-238	82-226	82-238
		Mean b	3.085	2.924	3.004	3.01	3.104	3.057
		SD	0.124	0.127	0.001	0.011	0.003	0.004
		r^2	0.967	0.972	0.970	0.977	0.961	0.969
	Monsoon	*NS*	118	197	315	112	109	221
		LR (mm)	69-316	108-296	69-316	66-179	93-309	66-309
		Mean b	3.023	3.011	3.017	3.011	2.908	2.959
		SD	0.001	0.008	0.004	0.005	0.132	0.068
		r^2	0.982	0.941	0.962	0.968	0.953	0.961
	Post-Monsoon	*NS*	134	148	282	143	86	249
		LR (mm)	82-174	72-217	72-217	69-215	88-307	69-307
		Mean b	2.994	3.108	3.051	3.046	2.998	3.022
		SD	0.025	0.006	0.009	0.077	0.006	0.042
		r^2	0.982	0.957	0.970	0.976	0.946	0.961

(Contd…)

	Period	Parameter	Central Sector			Northern Sector		
			M	*F*	*Both*	*M*	*F*	*Both*
J. setifer	**Pre-Monsoon**	*NS*	52	37	89	41	29	70
		LR (mm)	52-106	63-125	52-125	71-125	57-131	57-131
		Mean b	2.902	2.993	2.947	2.899	3.041	2.97
		SD	0.015	0.028	0.021	0.017	0.065	0.041
		r^2	0.964	0.958	0.961	0.942	0.955	0.949
	Monsoon	*NS*	109	132	241	31	67	98
		LR (mm)	66-127	57-109	57-127	61-133	86-118	61-133
		Mean b	2.941	2.975	2.958	2.861	2.975	2.918
		SD	0.077	0.037	0.057	0.01	0.03	0.02
		r^2	0.964	0.913	0.939	0.978	0.943	0.961
	Post-Monsoon	*NS*	104	86	190	67	104	171
		LR (mm)	46-101	51-89	46-101	55-122	63-116	55-122
		Mean b	2.862	2.726	2.794	2.889	2.77	2.829
		SD	0.049	0.043	0.046	0.019	0.077	0.048
		r^2	0.983	0.963	0.973	0.955	0.949	0.952

(M-male, F-female, NS- number of samples, SD - standard deviation, r^2-regression cofeeicient)

northern sector (2.959). In pre-monsoon, the value was 3.031as a whole and 3.057 was maximum estimated in northern sector and 3.004 in central sector. Similarly in post-monsoon season, the value was highest in central sector (3.051) followed by northern sector (3.022) and 3.037 as a whole. So the calculated b value was highest in post monsoon season followed by pre-monsoon season and in monsoon it was lowest (2.988). The growth variation also calculated in different season in separate sexes. In case of male the calculated b value was highest in pre-monsoon season (3.048) followed by post-monsoon (3.02) and lowest in monsoon season (3.017). In female, the value was maximum in post-monsoon (3.053) followed by pre-monsoon (3.014) and monsoon season (2.96).

In *J. setifer*, the estimated b value was 2.9 (seasonal SD ±.092) in central sector, 2.906 (seasonal SD ±.071) in northern sector and 2.903 as a whole. In seasonal variation, the estimated value was highest in pre-monsoon season (2.959) followed by monsoon (2.938) and lowest in post-monsoon season (2.812). In sectoral variation, the northern sector in monsoon season was highest value (2.97) and lowest 2.794 in central sector in post-monsoon season. The b value for male was 2.901 for both pre-monsoon and monsoon season and 2.876 in post-monsoon season. Similarly for female the value was 3.017, 2.975 and 2.748 in pre-monsoon, monsoon and post-monsoon respectively. So here we found that the growth value was highest in pre-monsoon season for both the sexes.

From the above result it was clear that the maximum growth of *R. sarba* was found in central sector (3.024) than in northern sector. The central sector is brackish water zone and the more productive Nalabana bird sanctuary is there. The sanctuary is the largest bird gathering zone in Asia and the nursery and breeding ground of many fishes and shell-fishes. This is because the nitrogenous west excreta are playing the major role to grow different types of vegetation, which is preferably best area for food and shelter of many fishes. As *R. sarba* is a brackish water species (Mohapatra *et.al.*,2007), such type of brackish environment facilitates better saline condition and suitable diet composition which is very necessary for growth of the species. As a brackish-marine species, *J. setifer* also prefer central sector and here the growth is higher than the northern sector, which is completely a fresh water zone. In case of female, *R. sarba* having the more growth rate as estimated in central sector than in northern sector but in *J. setifer*, female prefers fresh zone more followed by brackish zone. Male of *R. sarba* having the high growth rate than the female but in case of *J. setifer* it was reverse i.e., female is more growing type than male. This is clear from the length variation also, which were caught for the experiment in different time from different places. Because the maximum length of male *R. sarba* species (316mm) caught in central sector in monsoon season but the female having highest length was only 303mm in northern sector in monsoon season. In case of *J. setifer* the female having higher length caught in pre-monsoon season (northern sector) whereas 127mm only for male in monsoon season (central sector). In breeding season, the female gains more weight, as their gonad weight increase rapidly. So in central sector, females of *R. sarba* having more growth rate whereas the females of *J. setifer* grow rapidly in northern sector (monsoon season).

Finally the calculated 'b' value of *R. sarba* and *J. setifer*, were within the limits reported by Royce (1972), Carlander (1969) and Lagler *et al.*, (1977) for most fishes. In general, b values of fish are closer to 3, despite the many variations of fish forms (Cinco, 1982; King, 1996). According to Jones (1976) the LWR may change seasonally. Such variations in *b* values can be attributed to the combination of one or more of the following factors:

(a) differences in the number of specimen examined;

(b) area/season effect; and

(c) differences in the observed length ranges of the specimen caught (Gokhan et al., 2007).

So here the present values may be considered as average one. Even though the change of *b* values depends primarily on the shape and fatness of the species, various factors may be responsible for the differences in parameters of the length-weight relationships among seasons and years, such as temperature, salinity, food (quantity, quality and size), sex and time of year and stage of maturity (Pauly, 1984; Sparre Venema, 1992). According to Gonçalves *et al.* (1997), and Ozaydin Taskavak, (2007), the parameter *b*, unlike the parameter *a*, may vary seasonally, and even daily, and between habitats. Thus, the length-weight relationship in fish is affected by a number of factors including gonad maturity, sex, diet, stomach fullness and health as well as season and habitat (Mourad *et al.*, 2008), none of which were taken into consideration in the present study.

The growth rate of *Rhabdosargus sarba* and *Jerreomorpha setifer* was estimated from the length-weight relationship (LWR) only for the commercial value of the species. This study will helpful for the researcher those are interested to do more study on the above two species later. Some more related study also required to know about the breeding season, spawning and nursery ground, so that we can reach in a certain conclusion which can helpful to implement the fishing activities, methods and management plan for these two commercially important fish species in the Asia's largest brackish water lagoon.

REFERENCES

Amin, S. M.N., Zafar, M. and Halim, A. (2008). Age, Growth, Mortality and Population Structure of the Oyster, Crassostrea Madrasensis, in the Moheskhali Channel (Southeastern Coast of Bangladesh). *J. Appl. Ichthyol.* 24: 18-25.

Anderson, R. and Gutreuter, S. (1983). Length, Weight, and Associated Structural Indices. *Fisheries Techniques* (ed. Nielsen L, Johnson D.). American Fisheries Society. p. 283-300.

Beverton, R.J.H. and Holt S. J. (1996). *On the Dynamics of Exploited Fish Populations.* Chapman and Hall, London.

Bhatta, K.S., Pattnaik, A.K., Behera, B.P. (2001). Further Contribution to the Fish Fauna of Chilika Lagoon—A Coastal Wetland of Orissa. *GIOBIOS.* 28(2-3): 97-100.

Boehlert, G.W. and Mundy, B.C. (1988). Roles of Behavioural and Physical Factors in Larval and Juvenile Fish Recruitment to Estuarine Nursery Areas. *American Fisheries Society Symposium.* 3: 51-67.

Bolger, T., and Connoly, P.L. (1989). The selection of Suitable Indices for the Measurement and Analysis of Fish Condition. *J. Fish Biol.* 34: 171-182.

Carlander, K. (1969). *Handbook of Freshwater Fishery Biology.* Vol. 1. Iowa State University Press, Ames, Iowa.

Chaudhuri, B.L. (1916a). Description of Two New Fishes from Chilika Lake. *Rec. Indian Mus.* 12(3): 105-108.

Chaudhuri, B.L. (1916b). Fauna of the Chilika Lake: Fish Part I. *Mem. Indian Mus.* 5(4): 403-440.

Chaudhuri, B.L. (1916c). Fauna of the Chilika Lake: Fish Part II. *Mem. Indian Mus.* 5(5): 441-458.

Chaudhuri, B.L. (1917). Fauna of the Chilika Lake: Fish Part III. *Mem. Indian Mus.* 5(6): 491-508.

Cinco, E. (1982). Length-weight Relationship of Fishes in Small Scale Fisheries of San Miguel Bay, Philippines. *Biology and Stock Assessment. ICLARM Tech. Rep.* (ed. D. Pauly and A.N. Mines). 7 : 34-37.

Fafioye, O.O. and Oluajo, O. A. (2005). Length-weight Relationships of Five Fish Species in Epe Lagoon, Nigeria. *African Journal of Biotechnology.* 4(7): 749-751.

Ferhat, Kalayci, Necati, Samsun, Sabri, Bilgin, Osman, Samsun. (2007). Length-Weight Relationship of 10 Fish Species Caught by Bottom Trawl and Midwater Trawl from the Middle Black Sea, Turkey. *Turkish Journal of Fisheries and Aquatic Sciences.* 7:33-36.

Gokhan Gokce, Ilker Aydýn and Cengiz Metin. (2007). Length–weight Relationships of 7 Fish Species from the North Aegean Sea, Turkey. *International Journal of Natural and Engineering Sciences.* 1: 51-52.

Gonçalves, J. M. S., Bentes, L., Lino, P. G., Ribeiro, J., Canario, A. V. M. & Erzini, K. (1997). Weight-length Relationships for Selected Fish Species of the Small-scale Demersal Fisheries of the South and South-west Coast of Portugal. *Fisheries Research.* 30: pp. 253-256.

Jones, R. (1976). Growth of Fishes, *In* D.H. Cushing and J.J. Walsh (eds.) *The Ecology of the Seas.* Blackwell Scientific Publications, Oxford. 251-279.

King, R.P. (1996). Length-weight Relationships of Nigerian Freshwater Fishes, Naga. *ICLARM* Q. 19(3): 49-52.

Kolher, N., Casey, J. & Turner, P. (1995). Lengthweight Relationships for 13 Species of Sharks from the Western North Atlantic. *Fishery Bulletin.* 93: 412-418.

Lagler, K.F., J.E. Bardach, R.R. Miller and D.R.M. Assino. (1977). *Ichthyology* (2nd ed.) Wiley and Sons, New York, 506p.

Lobry, J., Mourand, L., Rochard, E. and Elie, P. (2003). Structure of the Gironde Estuarine Fish Assemblages: A Comparison of European Estuaries Perspective. *Aquatic Living Resources*. 16: 47.58.

Miller, J. M and Dunn, M. L. (1980). Feeding Strategies and Patterns of Movement in Juvenile Estuarine Fishes. In: *Estuarine Perspective*. (ed. V.S. Kennedy). Academic Press. 437-481.

Mohapatra, A., Mohanty R. K., Mohanty S. K., Bhatta K. S., Das N. R. (2007). Fisheries Enhancement and Biodiversity Assessment of Fish, Prawn and Mud Crab in Chilika Lagoon Through Hydrological Intervention. *Wetlands Ecol. Manage*. 15: 229-251.

Monteleone, D.M. (1992). Seasonality and Abundance of Ichthyoplankton in Great South Bay, New York. *Estuaries*. 15(2): 230-238.

Morato, T.P., Afonso, P., Lourinho, P., Barreiros, J.P., Santos, R.S. & Nash, R.D.M. (2001). Length-weight Relationships for 21 Coastal Fish Species of the Azores, North-eastern Atlantic. *Fisheries Research*. 50: 297-302.

Mourad, Cherif, Rafik Zarrad, Houcine Ghabri, Hechmi Missaoui and Othman Jarboui. (2008). Length-weight Relationships for 11 Fish Species from the Gulf of Tunis (SW Mediterranean Sea, Tunisia). *Pan-American Journal of Aquatic Sciences*. 3(1): 1-5

Oliva-Paterna, F.J., Andreu, A., Miñano, P.A., Verdiell, D., Egea, A., de Maya, J. A., Ruiz-Navarro, A., Garcia- Alonso, J., Fernández-Delgado, C. and Torralva, M. (2006). Y-O-Y Fish Species Richness in the Littoral Shallows of the Meso-saline Coastal Lagoon (Mar Menor, Mediterranean Coast of the Iberian Peninsula). *Journal of Applied Ichthyology*. 22: 235-237.

Ozaydin, O. and Taskavak, E. (2007). Length-weight Relationships for 47 Fish Species from Izmir Bay (Eastern Agean Sea, Turkey). *Acta Adriatica*. 47(2): 211-216.

Pauly, D. (1984). *Fish Population Dynamics in Tropical Waters: A Manual for Use with Programmable Calculators*. ICLARM Studies and Reviews 8. ICLARM, Manila, Philippines. p. 325.

Perez-Ruzafa, A., Quispe-Becerra, J. I., Garcia-Charton, J. A. and Marcos, C. (2004). Composition, Structure and Distribution of the Ichthyoplankton in a Mediterranean Coastal Lagoon. *Journal of Fish Biology*. 64: 202-218.

Petrakis, G. & Stergiou, K. I. (1995). Weight Length Relationships for 33 Fish Species in Greek Waters. *Fisheries Research*. 21: 465-469.

Repeeka, R. (2003). The Species Composition of the Ichthyofauna in the Lithuanian Economic Zone of the Baltic Sea and the Curonian Lagoon and its Changes in Recent Years. *Acta Zoologica Lituanica*. 13(2): 149-157.

Royce, W. F. (1972). Introduction to Fishery Sciences. *Academic Press, London*. p. 35.

Rozas L.P., Odum W.E. (1998). Occupation of Submerged Aquatic Vegetation by Fishes: Testing the Roles of Food and Refuge. *Oecologia, 77*: 101-106.

Sparre, P. and Venema, S.C. (1992). *Introduction to Tropical Fish Stock Assessment*. Part I: Manual. FAO Fisheries Technical Paper. p. 376.

Stergiou, K.I. & Moutopoulos, D. K. 2001. A Review of Length-weight Relationships of Fishes from Greek Marine Waters. Naga, ICLARM Quart. 24(1-2): 23-39.

Ustups, Didzis, Evalds Urtans, Atis Minde, Danute Uzars. 2003. The Structure and Dynamics of Fish Communities in the Latvian Coastal zone (Pape - Pçrkone), Baltic Sea. Acta Universitatis Latviensis, 662: 33-44.

Yoklavich, M. M.; Stevenson, M. and Cailliet, G. M. (1992). Seasonal and Spatial Patterns of Chthyoplankton Abundance in Elkhorn Slough, California. *Estuarine, Coastal and Shelf Science*. 34/35: 1-21.

13

Isolation and Characterization of *Bacillus sphaericus* from *Anopheles* Larva

S.N. Chatterjee,[1] Das D.,[1] T. Sen,[2] and K. Das[2]

ABSTRACT

Non-toxic *Bacillus sphaericus* was isolated from the gut of *Anopheles* larva. The colonies were circular, white, flat and undulate. Organisms were positive for Gram stain, spore and crystal staining. The isolate showed its salt-tolerant nature. The organisms failed to grow anaerobically. Bacteria didn't produce acid and gas from carbon source. The bacteria were positive for protease and lipase activities. Organisms were found to sensitive to chloramphenicol, kanamycin, eryrthromycin, ofloxacin, lomefloxacin, tobramycin, doxycycline, gatifloxacin, amikacin, gentamycin, sparfloxacin, cefadroxil. This strain survived as normal flora of larval gut of *Anopheles* mosquito.

1. Department of Zoology, Burdwan University, Burdwan - 713104, West Bengal.

2. Microbiology Department, Rabindra Mahavidyalaya, Hooghly, West Bengal.

INTRODUCTION

The class Insecta consists of a large group of organisms with rich species diversity. There are an estimated 750,000 species of insects, but the actual number could be far more than this as some regions have been poorly studied and many ecosystems, especially in the tropics, have not been explored at all. Some estimates put the number as high as 10 million (Novotny *et al* 2002). All insect species are known to harbour a rich and complex community of microorganisms in their guts and other body regions. This microbiota participates in many types of interactions ranging from pathogenesis to obligate mutualism (Dillon and Dillon, 2004). One reason for the microbial diversity is that different groups of insects have different feeding habits; this results in different gut structures and functions and promotes the establishment of different phylotypes. There has been renewed interest in the understanding of insect gut microorganisms for two reasons. First, this diverse microbiota is a potential source of novel bioactive compounds such as antimalarial, antiviral and antitumour peptides (Chernysh *et al.*, 2002), enzymes (Zhang and Brune 2004) and novel metabolites (Wilkinson 2001). Second, manipulating these microbial symbionts is thought to be an effective strategy for controlling the spread of pathogens that use insects as hosts (Mickes and Ferguson, 1961; Lehane, *et al.*, 1997; Beard, *et al.*, 2002; Dillon *et al.*, 2005). It appears that insect guts are reservoirs for a large variety of microbes. Many are poorly characterized and considering the diversity of insects, there must be novel microbes awaiting discovery. Our understanding of the biology of insects will be incomplete without a comprehensive understanding of their gut microbes, as these have a significant impact on various life processes of the hosts. While the roles of endosymbionts like *Wolbachia* and *Buchnera* are better understood, not much is known about the normal microbial community flora. Characterization of midgut microbes using molecular tools is the first step in understanding their role in insect biology. Mosquitoes are important vectors of disease, carrying numerous maladies ranging from dengue to lymphatic filiariasis to malaria. While insecticides are the method of choice for mosquito control, its widespread use has resulted in resistant mosquitoes. Thus, other ways to control the mosquito population must be found. Although the life cycle of each pathogen is different, all must survive ingestion, exposure to the midgut, and migration to the salivary glands for transmission to a new host. If the pathogen cannot survive one of these steps, the mosquito cannot transfer the disease (Beerntsen *et al.*, 2000). This presents a new angle to mosquito control. Instead of controlling the mosquito population, one may be able to control the ability of the mosquito to transmit pathogens. This may release the selective pressure on mosquitoes to become resistant to control methods. The midgut presents several barriers to pathogen transmission including dodging the mosquito's digestive enzymes, escaping the peritrophic matrix, and infecting and escaping from the gut epithelial cells (Beerntsen *et al.*, 2000.) Not much is known about the microbial flora associated with the mosquito midgut and whether it might be involved in blocking the ability of the pathogen from infecting the gut epithelium (Straif *et al.*, 1998). Also, the gut flora may contain ideal candidates to be genetically modified to produce anti-pathogen compounds (paratransgenesis). Present study has been designed to isolate and characterize the bacterial flora of midgut of *Anopheles* mosquito. Present study is an attempt to isolate and characterize the gut flora of *Anopheles* larvae.

MATERIALS AND METHODS

Mosquito Species

The *Anopheles* mosquito species used in the experiments were obtained from laboratory colonies maintained at the Microbiology research unit, Parasitology and Microbiology Laboratory, Department of Zoology, Burdwan University, Burdwan. The mosquitoes were maintained at a temperature of 28°C (±2° C) and relative humidity of 80 (± 5%).

Bacteria Isolation

A single larva was washed in 70% alcohol and the gut contents were inoculated in the nutrient agar medium. The Petri plate was incubated in the BOD incubator for 24 hours. After the incubation, there were visible bacterial colonies. This bacterial culture was maintained regularly. Morphological characters of the colonies and the bacteria were studied following the standard microbiological methods (Collee and Miles, 1989; Lacey, 1997).

CHARACTERIZATION OF THE ISOLATED BACTERIA

Morphological Characters

Morphological characters of the colonies and the bacteria were studies following the standard microbiological methods (Collee and Miles, 1989; Lacey, 1997). The isolates were dilution streaked on NA plates, incubated for 72 hours at 30 ± 0.1° C. The shape, size, colour, margin and opacity were recorded from isolated colonies. The isolates were streaked on NA slants and stab cultured with a straight needle pierced through the centre of the NA stab tubes, incubated at 30 ± 0.1° C for 72 hours and growth of the organism were recorded. Morphology of the vegetative cells, spores and crystals were observed under a phase-contrast microscope under a 100X objective from <18 hours (for vegetative cells and motility) and ≥ 5 days old (spores and crystals) cultures grown on NA plates at 30 ± 0.1°C in a BOD incubator. Staining characters of the organism were studied for vegetative, reproductive and crystal structure determination. To study the Gram's stain (crystal violet) i. e. Gram (+ve) or Gram (-ve) characters of the isolates, dilute suspensions of the bacteria were smeared on clean slides, air dried, heat fixed by passing over a flame for 2-3 times. The slides were flooded with crystal violet solution for one minute, washed with water and flooded with Gram's iodine for one minute. The slides were washed with water and decolorized with 95% ethyl alcohol dropped from a dropping bottle until no violet colour was visible from drain off alcohol. The slides were washed with water and counter stained with safranin stain for about 30 seconds and washed with water.

The slides were air-dried and examined under a microscope using 100X objective using a daylight filter. For staining spores and crystal bacterial cultures of >5 days old were preferred. For spore and crystal staining, small amount of bacterial suspensions were smeared on a oil free clean slides. The slide was air-dried and heat fixed over a flame. The spores were stained with malachite green stain. The smear was flooded with the stain, steamed (avoid boiling) over a flame for 10 minutes, washed under tap water, counter stained with safranin and observed under 100X objective. The spores take green stain.

BIOCHEMICAL CHARACTERS

Indole Production

In the presence of oxygen, some bacteria are able to split tryptophan (by tryptophanase) into indole and alpha-aminopropionic acid. The presence of indole can be detected by the addition of Ehrlich's Kovac's reagent (p-dimetyl-amino-benzaldehyde) and is indicated by the formation of a red colored ring (a condensation product formed as a result of reaction between pyrrole structure of indole and p-dimetyl-amino-benzaldehyde in acidic environment) soluble in ether, chloroform and alcohol. The test was performed by inoculating fresh culture in 1% (w/v) tryptone broth, after growth, 0.2 ml of Kovac's reagent (p-dimethylamino benzaldehyde, 5 g; amyl alcohol, 75 ml; conc. HCl, 25 ml) was added and the mixture was shaken well. Positive reaction was indicated by appearance of deep red to pink color in the reagent layer.

Catalase Activity

Catalase is a metalloprotein that breaks down hydrogen peroxide, the toxic byproduct of respiratory metabolism. To detect presence of catalase, a freshly grown culture was taken and few drops of 3% H_2O_2 were added to it. This qualitative assay was done on both agar plate and on slide. Bacterial strains capable of producing catalase will produce intensive bubbling due to release of oxygen produced due to breakdown of H_2O_2 into oxygen and water. Weak catalase positive strain produces less or small bubbles, which were seen under stereomicroscope.

Nitrate Reduction

The test was performed by growing the bacterial strain on nitrate broth (beef extract, 0.3 %; peptic digest of animal tissue, 0.5 %; potassium nitrate, 0.1 %; ph 7.2 ± 0.2) or on MMR2A broth supplemented with 0.1 % potassium nitrate (depending upon strain) followed by addition of equal amounts of nitrate reagent A (0.8 g sulphanilic acid in 100ml of 5N acetic acid) and B (0.5 g a-naphthylamine in 100ml of 5N acetic acid). Reduction of nitrate to nitrite was indicated by red or pink color (due to formation of diazonium compound as a result of reaction between nitrite and naphthylamine). No color change indicates that nitrate is not at all reduced or it has been reduced to nitrite and then to nitrogen gas. To validate that nitrate was not reduced at all, Zn dust is added (after addition of nitrate reagents) which chemically reduces nitrate (if any left in the medium) to nitrite, the latter then reacts as stated earlier to give pink or red coloration. Nitrogen gas on the other hand could be recorded by accumulation of air in the Durham's tube, which was kept in the nitrate broth.

Acid Production from Carbohydrate

Acid production from different carbohydrates was checked on basal medium, which lacked any carbon source. Carbon free basal medium (w/v, Ammonium sulphate, 0.2 %, K_2HPO_4, 0.024 %; $MgSO_4.7H_2O$, 0.024 %; KCl, 0.01 %; yeast extract, 0.01 %; bromocresol purple or phenol red, 0.004 %, pH, 7.2 ± 0.2) was used for this test. Each carbohydrate was filtered sterilized and was used at a concentration of 0.5 % (w/v).

Gas Production from Glucose

This was checked on dextrose broth (%, w/v, beef extract, 0.3, tryptose, 1; dextrose, 0.5; NaCl, 0.5; phenol red as indicator) with a Durham's tube for gas accumulation. Gas production was indicated by accumulation of air within Durham's tube while acid production was indicated by change in colour of broth from red to yellow due to lowering of pH.

Citrate Utilization

This was checked on Simmon's citrate agar (%, w/v; $MgSO_4.7H_2O$, 0.02; ammonium dihydrogen phosphate, 0.1; dipotassium phosphate, 0.1; sodium citrate, 0.2; NaCl, 0.5; bromo thymol blue, 0.008; agar, 1.5; pH 6.8 ± 0.2). Bacterial strains capable of utilizing citrate as sole source of carbon and energy grew well and produced a color shift from greenish to blue due to alkaline pH of the medium that was created as citrate is utilized.

Oxidase Activity

Cytochrome c is the terminal component in the electron transport chain of respiratory metabolism of organism. In its oxidized state it takes up electron and pass on to oxygen (terminal acceptor). The reduced cytochrome is then further oxidized by oxidase and the cycle continues. This test was performed by using oxidase reagent (N, N, N', N'-tetramethyl-p-phenylenediamine) which acts as the artificial electron donor. Under reduced state it is colourless but when it is oxidized (and the electron is transferred to cytochrome c) it becomes purplish in color. To a thin smear of fresh culture on a slide or to a fresh culture on an agar plate, added few drops of aqueous solution of oxidase reagent (a pinch in 5 ml water), if the color changes from colorless to purple within 5-10 seconds it indicated a positive reaction, color development after 30 sec indicated delayed positive. If no color change was observed in more than 30 sec then the strain was considered negative.

Gelatin Hydrolysis

Plate based method: Bacterial strains were inoculated onto Nutrient agar supplemented with 0.4% gelatin. After good growth has appeared on the plate, it was flooded with gelatin-precipitating reagent (15 % $HgCl_2$ in 20 % concentrated HCl). Clear zones around colonies indicated a positive hydrolysis.

Starch Hydrolysis

To perform this test starch agar (all in % w/v, peptic digest of animal tissue, 0.5; yeast extract, 0.15; beef extract, 0.15; soluble starch, 0.2; NaCl, 0.5; agar, 1.5) supplemented with 0.2% soluble starch (depending upon the nature of the strain) was used. After 2 to 4 days of growth, the plate was flooded with Gram's iodine. A clear zone (where starch was depleted) in the background of blue colour (where starch is not depleted) indicated positive reaction of hydrolysis.

MR-VP (Methyl Red-Voges Poskauer) Test

Both these tests are performed on MR-VP broth (buffered peptone, 0.7%; dextrose, 0.5%; Dipotassium phosphate, 0.5 %; pH 6.9 ± 0.2). Oxidative metabolism of glucose leads to accumulation of acid, lowering the pH of the medium, a positive MR test indicates the pH of 4.5 or lower due to production of mixed acid fermentation. After suitable period (2, 3, 5 and 7 days) of growth on MR-VP broth, MR test was performed by adding few drops of Methyl red (0.1g methyl red in 300 ml of 95% ethanol, make upto 500ml with distilled water) reagent. A positive test was indicated by red coloration.The VP test, detects Acetoin (acetylmethylcarbinol or 2, 3 butanediol), which is produced during glucose metabolism. This test was performed by adding 0.4 ml of 40% KOH solution to 2 to 7-day old culture in MR-VP broth, followed by addition of a pinch of creatinine. A positive reaction was indicated by appearance of red to pink colour (condensation product formed due to KOH mediated oxidation of acetoin, which in turn reacts with guanidine nuclei, present in arginine and other peptone constituents).

Lipase Activity

Lipolytic activity was checked by determination of hydrolysis of Tween 80 (polyethylene sorbitan monooleate). The test medium consisted of basal medium (w/v, peptone, 1%; NaCl, 0.5%; $CaCl_2.H_2O$, 0.01%; agar, 1.5%) supplemented with 1% Tween 80. Positive hydrolysis was indicated by appearance of opaque zones (due to Ca-salt of cleaved oleic acid) around the growth.

Tween 20

Hydrolysis of Tween 20 (polyoxyethylene sorbitan monolaurate), Tween 40 (polyoxyethylene sorbitan monopalmitate) and Tween 60 (polyoxyethylene sorbitan monostearate) were also checked using the same medium and procedure as described above.

Antibiotic Snsitivity Test for the Organisms

Response of the organism to different antibiotics was tested on NA medium. The NA plates were surface seeded with concentrated bacterial suspension. Different antibiotic discs with effective concentrations were placed over the plates. Inhibition of growth depicted by a clear zone formation around the discs indicated sensitive reaction otherwise the organism was resistant to the antibiotic. Diameter of the inhibition zone was measured with an antibiotic zone scale. Ratio of the inhibition zone and disc area produced the activity level of the antibiotics.

RESULTS AND DISCUSSION

The gut of many insects contains a bactericidal principle of unknown nature which greatly restricts the bacterial flora, and the flora is limited to a few kinds of aerobic Bacilli. These are non-proteolytic and therefore of no importance in digestion (Wigglesworth, 1977). The most commonly occurring micro-organismsin in insects are bacteria or bacterium like forms which are found in Blattaria, Isoptera, Homoptera, Heteroptera, Anoplura, Mallophaga, Coleoptera, Hymenoptera, and Diptera (Chapman, 1973). One reason for the microbial diversity is that different groups of insects have different feeding habits resulting in different gut structures and functions and promotes the establishment of different phylotypes. The colony characters of the bacterial isolates under study were circular, white, flat and undulate (Table 13.1). The bacteria were gram-positive in nature. The characteristics of vegetative cells, spores and crystals of isolates are given in Tables 13.1 and 13.2. Length of the organisms ranged from 1.75-2.7 ìm and diameter from 0.41-0.66 μm. All the bacteria were positive for Gram stain, spore and crystal staining (Table 13.2 and 13.3).The bacterum tolerated up to 8% NaCl (Table 13.4) revealing the salt-tolerant nature of this isolate. The organisms failed to grow anaerobically. Acid and gas production were not achieved from carbon sources by these bacteria (Table 13.5). The physiological and biochemical properties of standard cultures are presented in Table 13.6.The organisms were catalase positive, indole positive, citrate positive, nitrate reduction negative, Vogues-Proskauer test negative, Urease production test, Oxidase positive and H_2S Production test negative. The bacteria were positive for protease and lipase activities (Table 13.7). Response of the organisms to the recommended doses of different antibiotics (Table 13.8) showed that all of them were sensitive to chloramphenicol, kanamycin, eryrthromycin, ofloxacin, lomefloxacin, tobramycin, doxycycline, gatifloxacin, amikacin, gentamycin, sparfloxacin, cefadroxil, but resistant to PenicillinG, tetracycline, ampicillin, ciprofloxacin, norfloxacin, nalidixic acid, cefuroxine and levofloxacin. On the basis of morphological and biochemical characters this bacterial isolate was identified as *Bacillus sphaericus*. These organisms survived in the gut of *Anopheles* larvae without causing any harmful effects, rather as normal flora of larval gut.

Table 13.1: Colony characters

Bacteria No.	*Form*	*Colour*	*Elevation*	*Margin*
Bs-7	Circular	white	Flat	Entire

Table 13.2: Characteristics of vegetative cells

Bacteria No.	*Shape*	*Length(µm)*		*Breath(µm)*		*Motility*	*Gram stain*
		Range	*Mean*	*Range*	*Mean*		
Bs-7	Rods with rounded ends	1.75-2.7	2.17	0.41-0.66	0.59	Motile	+

Table 13.3: Characters of spores of isolate:

Bacteria No.	*Shape*	*Spore stain*
Bs-7	Round	+

Table 13.4: Sodium chloride tolerance of the isolate

Medium	*Isolate No.*
	Bs-7
NA + Sodium chloride (%)	
1.	+
2.	+
3.	+
4.	+
5.	+
6.	+
7.	+
8.	+
10.	-

+ = Positive result.

- = Negative result

Table 13.5: Acid and gas production from carbon source

Carbon source	*Acid production*	*Gas production*
D-glucose	–	–
D-arabinose	–	–
D-xylose	–	–
D-Mannitol	–	–

- = Negative result.

Table 13.6: Some physiological and biochemical properties of isolates and standard culture

Tests	*Reaction*
Catalase	+
Indole production	+
Methyl red test	+
Vogues-Proskauer test	-
Nitrate reduction test	-
Urease production test	+
Oxidase	+
H_2S Production Test	-
Citrate Test	+

+ = Positive result.

- = Negative result.

Table 13.7: Enzymatic activities of standard cultures

Tests	*Reaction*
Protease	
Gelatin hydrolysis	+
Casein hydrolysis	+
Starch hydrolysis	–
Lipase hydrolysis	Weakly +

+ = Positive result.

- = Negative result.

Table 13.8: Antibiotic assay of the isolate

Antibiotics (μg/disc)	*Reaction*	*Clear Zone diameter (mm)*
Tetracycline (30)	R	0
Ampicillin (10)	R	0
Chloramphenicol (30)	S	13
Penicillin G (10)	R	0
Kanamycin (30)	S	14
Erythromycin (15)	S	24
Ciprofloxacin (5)	R	0
Ofloxacin (5)	S	15
Lomefloxacin (10)	S	18
Tobramycin (10)	S	21
Doxycyclin (30)	S	19
Nalidixic acid (30)	R	0
Gatifloxacin (10)	S	23
Amikacin (30)	S	18
Gentamycin (10)	S	14
Cefuroxime (30)	R	0
Levofloxacin (5)	R	0
Sparfloxacin (10)	S	16
Cefadroxil (30)	S	15

R-resistance;

S-sensitive.

REFERENCES

Beard, B C, Cordon-Rosales C and Durvasula R V 2002 Bacterial Symbionts of the Triaminae and Their Potential Use in Control of Chagas Disease Transmission; *Annu. Rev. Entomol.* 47: 123-141.

Beernstsen, B.T., James, A.A., and B.M. Christensen. 2000. Genetics of Mosquito Vector Competence. *Microbiology and Molecular Biology Reviews*. 64(1): 115-137.

Chapman, R.F., 1973 *The Insects-structure and Function*. The English Universities Press Ltd., St Paul's House, Warwick Lane, London. p. 819.

Chernysh, S, Kim S I, Bekker G, Pleskach V A, Filatova N A, Anikin V B, Platonov V G and Bulet P. 2002. Antiviral and Antitumor Peptides from Insects; *Proc. Natl. Acad. Sci. USA* 99 12628-12632.

Collee, J.G. and Miles P.S. 1989. Tests for Identification of Bacteria. In: Practical Medical Microbiology. (eds.) J.G. Collee, J.P. Duguid, A.G. Fraser, B.P. Marmion, Churchil Livingstone, NY, USA, p. 141-160.

Dillon R J, Vennard C T, Buckling A and Charnley A K 2005 Diversity of Locust Gut Bacteria Protects Against Pathogen Invasion; *Ecol. Lett.* 8 1291-1298.

Dillon, R.J., and V.M. Dillon. 2004. The Gut Bacteria of Insects: Nonpathogenicm Interactions. *Annual Review of Entomology*. 49: 71-92.

Lehane, M J, Wu D and Lehane S M 1997 Midgut Specific Immune Molecules are Produced by the Blood-sucking Insect *Stomoxys calcitrant*; *Proc. Natl. Acad. Sci. USA* 94 11502-11507.

Lacey, LA. (1997). Manual of Techniques in Insect Pathology. Acad.Press, NY, USA, p. 409.

Micks, D W and Ferguson M J 1961 Microorganisms Associated with Mosquitoes. III. Effect of Reduction in the Microbial Flora of *Culex fatigans* Wiedemann on the Susceptibility to *Plasmodium relictum* Grassi and Feletti; *J. Insect. Pathol.* 3 144-148.

Novotny, V, Basset Y, Miller S E, Weiblen G D, Bremer B, Cizek L and Drozd P 2002 Low Host Specificity of Herbivorous Insects in a Tropical Forest; *Nature (London)* 416: 841-844.

Straif, S.C., Mbogo, C.N.M., Toure, A.M., Walker, E.D., Kaufman, M., Toure, Y.T. and J.C. Beier. 1998. Midgut Bacteria in *Anopheles Gambiae* and *Anfunestus* (Diptera:Culicidae) from Kenya and Mali. *Journal of Medical Entomology*. 35(3):222-226. Abstract.

Wigglesworth, V.B. 1977. *The Principles of Insect Physiology*. English Language Book Society and Chapman and Hall. p. 827.

Wilkinson, T. 2001. Disloyalty and Treachery in Bug-swapping Shocker; *Trends Ecol. Evol.* 16: 659-661.

Zhang, H and Brune A 2004 Characterization of Partial Purification of Proteinases from Highly Alkaline Midgut of the Humivorous Larvae of *Pachnoda Ephippiata* (Coleoptera: Scarabaeidae); *Soil Biol. Biochem.* 36: 435-442.

Index

D

E

F